INSIDE THE BUBBLE

ULTIMATE GUIDE TO THE WORLD'S LARGEST RETIREMENT COMMUNITY

RYAN ERISMAN

Copyright © 2021 by Ryan Erisman

All rights reserved.

No part of this book may be reproduced in any form or by any electronic or mechanical means, including information storage and retrieval systems, without written permission from the author, except for the use of brief quotations in a book review.

The author has used best efforts in preparing this book, however no warranties as to the accuracy or completeness of the information provided herein are expressed or implied. The author is not qualified to render legal, tax, or financial advice and the reader should consult with proper professionals before acting upon the information in this book. The author disclaims any liability, loss, or risk that is incurred as a consequence of the use and application of the contents of this book, including but not limited to the use of the recommended services provided herein.

DISCLAIMERS

THE VILLAGES® is a federally registered trademark of Holding Company of The Villages, Inc.

Inside The Bubble is not affiliated with, or sponsored by, Holding Company of The Villages, Inc. or its affiliated entities.

References in this book to "The Villages" primarily refer to The Villages® community.

The marks SPANISH SPRINGS TOWN SQUARE, LAKE SUMTER LANDING MARKET SQUARE, BROWNWOOD PADDOCK SQUARE, BROWNWOOD, THE SHARON, PROPERTIES OF THE VILLAGES, THE VILLAGES GOLF CARS, and THE VILLAGES GROWN are also federally registered trademarks of Holding Company of The Villages, Inc.

ALSO BY RYAN ERISMAN

The Florida Retirement Handbook

The Florida Retirement Handbook includes information on 100+ of the best places and communities for retirement, the effects the coronavirus pandemic has had on the Florida retirement landscape, the safest places to retire in Florida, cost of living information, navigate the Florida homeowner's insurance minefield, and more.

CONTENTS

1. An Introduction to The Villages — 9
2. History of The Villages — 15
3. The Villages Today — 26
4. Why Has The Villages Been So Successful? — 34
5. Criticism: Books, Articles, and Documentaries — 39
6. Getting to Really Know The Villages — 48
7. Come for a Visit — 51
8. Finding a Rental — 54
9. Getting Around The Villages — 59
10. It's a Golf Cart Life — 66
11. Golf & Tennis — 74
12. Recreation — 83
13. Dining, Shopping, and Entertainment — 101
14. Healthcare — 115
15. Crime and Public Safety — 125
16. Politics — 131
17. Cost of Living — 135
18. Community Development Districts Explained — 147
19. Finding Your Home — 153
20. Paying for Your New Home — 166
21. Property, Flood, & Sinkhole Insurance — 169
22. Home Inspections and Warranties for Resales — 179
23. Walkthrough and Warranty for New Homes — 184
24. New Home and Resale Closing Process — 193
25. Things To Do Right After Moving Here — 197
26. Additional Resources — 203

1

AN INTRODUCTION TO THE VILLAGES

Welcome to another edition of *Inside The Bubble!* If you are a long-time reader, *welcome back*! I hope you find this book gets a little better with each update.

If you're new here and just starting to learn about The Villages, congratulations on taking the first step towards learning about the ins and outs of Florida's most popular retirement community. Thank you for allowing me to be your guide.

The Villages is a 55+ community located in Central Florida, about an hour northwest of Orlando.

The Villages is home to more than 130,000 people, has more than 700 holes of golf, 200 pickleball courts, 100 recreation centers, 100 swimming pools, more than 3,000 clubs and organizations residents can participate in, an "enrichment academy" to support lifelong learning, more than 100 restaurants, a wide range of shops, grocery stores, and medical offices, free live entertainment on a nightly basis, and to top it off, nearly everything is golf cart accessible.

With all of that in mind, it's no wonder The Villages typically sells more than 2,000 new homes each year.

Yes, The Villages is an incredible place, but I must warn you that it is not for everyone. Thousands of people buy and move here every year, but thousands more take a close look and decide it's not for them. I hope this book plays a role in helping you decide if it's right for you.

Lay of the Land

The Villages is a huge place and it definitely takes newcomers some time to get the lay of the land.

Top to bottom, The Villages currently measures about 14 miles long and its about 5 miles across at its widest point.

One of the best ways for newcomers to get it into their minds how The Villages is laid out is to think of it as a long vertical rectangle with a lot of jagged edges. It's also important to note that The Villages has pretty much been (and continues to be) developed from north to south, so for the most part, the further south you go, the newer the homes and amenities tend to be.

Map is for illustrative purposes only

In addition to thinking of The Villages as a long vertical rectangle, there are four distinct areas ... three with town squares... and some major roadways running East to West that help us mentally or visually break it down further into sections.

Please keep in mind that the sections I'm about to describe are not "officially" recognized sections, but I came up with this way of describing the various parts of The Villages years ago and people seem to find it helpful.

I find that it helps newcomers when they think of The Villages as having four distinct areas:

Spanish Springs Area: Everything North of County Road 466

This area is the oldest part of The Villages. Spanish Springs, which was the first town square built in The Villages, is located in this section. Other major shopping centers nearby include La Plaza Grande Shopping Center, Rolling Acres Plaza, Spanish Plaines, Mulberry Grove Plaza, Buffalo Ridge and Southern Trace Shopping Centers.

The Savannah, Paradise, and La Hacienda Regional Recreation Complexes as well as several smaller recreation centers are also located in this area, along with The Villages Polo Club, Veterans Memorial Park, the Saddlebrook softball complex, and The Villages Regional Hospital.

Lake Sumter Landing Area: Everything Between County Road 466 and 466-A

This area includes the second town square built in The Villages, Lake Sumter Landing. Other points of interest include The Villages Charter School, The Villages High School, the Buffalo Glen Softball Complex, Laurel Manor, Colony Cottage, Lake Miona, and SeaBreeze Regional Recreation Complexes, and Colony Plaza Shopping Center.

Brownwood Area: Everything Between 466-A and State Road 44

This area includes the third town square, Brownwood Paddock Square, as well as the Brownwood Hotel and Spa, the Center for Advanced Healthcare at Brownwood, and The Villages' first apartment complex called the Lofts at Brownwood. Other highlights include The Eisenhower and Rohan Regional Recreation Complexes, The Villages Public Library, the Sharon Rose Weichens Preserve, the Soaring Eagle Softball Complex, and more.

New and Future Areas: Everything South of State Road 44

For years it was believed that The Villages would stop at State Road 44, but one thing you will learn about The Villages is that there's no use trying to predict what will happen here, even if that's based on official statements from the developer.

Over the last few years, The Villages has acquired enough land in this area south of State Road 44 to essentially double the size of the community. I don't believe we've quite settled the debate as to what this area will be referred to in the long run. Right now some call it "Southern Oaks" after the name of the large plat of land that takes up much of this area, some call it "Down South", and others are simply calling it "the new area". Maybe it will be called the "Eastport Area" if that lifestyle center turns out to be everything we think it will be.

But, for our purposes in this edition of the book, I'm just going to call it the "New and Future Areas" for now.

In 2020-21, three new bridges were added to the multi-modal path network to help golf carts, cyclists and pedestrians over the Florida Turnpike and SR 44 into this new area. Other similar bridges are planned to further connect the new and future areas of The Villages with the more established areas.

We'll talk more about all of the exciting new things on the horizon soon enough, but first, let's take a look at how we got here.

2
HISTORY OF THE VILLAGES

Like many pioneers and speculative businessmen before him, Harold Schwartz began development of The Villages as a result of one of the state's land booms.

The Florida sunshine has long been a draw, calling those who live in colder climates to move to the state. The rush for land began when Florida was still a territory, with cotton growers flocking to the panhandle, and settlers and seaport merchants populating the both coasts. In 1880, Florida's population was roughly 269,000, with people mostly in Jacksonville, Key West, Pensacola, Tallahassee, and Tampa.

Steamboats and Seminoles

When steamboats arrived on the scene in the early 1820s, they opened up the interior of the state for settlement. Florida's statehood in 1845 also drew more people to the area. Though some Northern naysayers doubted the value of Florida land beyond the St. Johns River (which runs parallel to the east coast, from Jacksonville to the central part of the state), tourism, and ensuing settlements, pushed west, beyond the river. By 1869, the steamers had found a path from the St. Johns all the way to Silver Springs, near Ocala (less than 25 mile from present day The Villages).

The first settlers in Marion County, one of the three counties The Villages occupies, came to the area in the 1840s for the free land being offered as part of the Armed Occupation Act. The act was passed as a way to populate the state and to control the Seminole Indians who were already occupying the land. The county was officially created in 1844, and until 1853, it included large parts of what are now Lake and Sumter counties.

By 1880, the State of Florida's budget was flagging. Its major asset was its nearly 200,000 acres of "swampland," which was put up for sale. Attracted by the potential offered by cheap land in the Sunshine State, Northern industrialist Hamilton Disston began snapping up the property. Eventually Disston owned four million Florida acres; roughly one-ninth of the state. Disston developed infrastructure for his land, which drew new residents to Florida en masse. This revitalized the state and paved the way for the railroads.

Railroads, largely built by Henry Flagler, ended the steamer era but further opened up the interior of the state. Rail service reached Marion County in 1881. Florida tourism blossomed. The Ocala area was at center stage with Silver Springs and its much-touted glass-bottomed boats. During this gilded age, tourists came to the state via opulent railcars and they wintered in magnificent resorts built by the railroad tycoon. This land boom lasted until the Panic of 1893, when over-building set off a series of bank failures.

The 1920s Boom and Beyond

As the end of World War I helped re-stabilize the economy, Florida's allure as an exotic paradise once again put the state in the real estate spotlight. With people like Miami investor Carl Fisher proclaiming, "It's June in Miami," land sales took off again in the 1920s and soared with the frenzy and electricity of the Jazz Age.

Fisher's promotional efforts called people to Florida, and his Dixie Highway, running from Indiana to Miami, made it easy for people to travel to the state in the newly popularized automobiles. Miami and South Florida saw great growth during the 1920s, but other real estate speculators saw the success of men like Fisher and set up land schemes of their own throughout the state.

Again, over-building and greed began to shatter the Florida real estate dream. By 1925 the northern press was warning people about sham Florida investments. If the press didn't drive the message home, the Miami Hurricane of 1926 did. The category-4 storm smacked the coast, devastating Miami and pushing Florida into Depression three years before the rest of the country.

Florida wouldn't begin to recover until after World War II. The next real estate boom wouldn't happen until the 1950s -- a time when enterprising men, such as Harold Schwartz, once again began touting Florida as a tropical oasis.

Mail Order and Retirees

After World War II, Americans had more money and more leisure time. Again the sunshine beckoned, this time calling those ready to retire. The construction of major Florida interstate highways and the invention of affordable, residential air conditioning made the move to Florida easier and more appealing than ever.

Like land sales in the 1920s, large chunks of pastureland were purchased by developers who, in turn, sold lots to Northerners hankering for a piece of paradise. Land was advertised "up North" and sold via mail order. Michigan businessman Harold Schwartz was among those selling the dream. Similar to others in the business, Schwartz sold land in Florida and New Mexico on the installment plan. A typical deal of the time - $10 down and $10 a month.

By the mid 1960s, retirement communities like Del Webb's Sun City, in Tampa, and the Century Villages, in south Florida, were flourishing. However, sales took a big hit in 1968 when Congress banned land sales by mail.

Still holding a lot of Florida land, in the early 1970s, Schwartz and partner, Al Tarrson, began work on Orange Blossom Gardens, a mobile home park in northwest Lake County. This wide spot in the middle of a pasture was the seed for what would become The Villages.

Orange Blossom Gardens

Schwartz and Tarrson labored with Orange Blossom Gardens during the 1970s, but by the early 1980's the community had only sold 400 homes. Wanting to turn things around, Schwartz bought out his partner and asked his son, Gary Morse, to help him with the business. Morse moved from Michigan to take over operations in 1983.

Realizing that communities like Sun City, (with a golf course, stocked ponds and hobby shops), were successful, in part, due to their amenities, the father-son team began to improve the development. Morse's wife, Sharon, also pitched in with her interior design skills. She upgraded the common areas and created a "style" for the buildings and homes in the community – a concept that plays an important part in the ambience of The Villages of today.

Orange Blossom Gardens grew, and soon began pushing the boundaries of the original mobile home park. Schwartz began to purchase and upgrade large tracts of land on the west side of Highway 441, in Sumter and Marion counties.

By 1985, Orange Blossom Gardens was annexed into the town of Lady Lake. By then fiestas were also being held in the community plaza and the development had two pools, horseshoe, bocce ball and tennis courts, and the front-nine of the Orange Blossom Hills golf course. Also that year, Schwartz's granddaughter, Jennifer Parr took over home sales.

Realizing that a successful community needed more than activities to keep its residents happy, the family developers began a plan to create a self-contained community that provided everything its residents would need. Gary's son,

Mark Morse, joined the team and began work on the first commercial and medical center, La Plaza Grande. The plaza drew a bank and a medical office, but to fill the plaza and lure more tenants, the family started and managed several businesses of their own. Orange Blossom Hills also began to design and manufacture their own homes.

By 1987 the development had $40 million in annual sales and more than $4 million in profits but growth continued. A bowling center and a grocery store moved in, and the size of the recreation department doubled. Home sales also flourished. The "village" neighborhood concept was created and the villages of Del Mar, El Cortez and Mira Mesa were built.

In the early 1990s, a golf course and the first recreation center were built on the new side of the highway. Orange Blossom Gardens got their first home-owned bank, and the first phase of La Hacienda Hotel was opened. Schwartz's second son, Richard joined on as golf director.

In less than a decade, Orange Blossom Gardens powered Lady Lake from a town of about 3,000 into a thriving city of more than 10,000.

The Villages

More neighborhood villages were built, and by 1991, the name of the development was changed to The Villages. Two key things propelled The Villages forward; the creation of the first town center and new form of financing called Community Development Districts (CDDs).

Community Development Districts are special-purpose local governments. They are structured so developers can control the "district" and issue low-interests bonds. Funds from the bonds are then used to build infrastructure and amenities for the district residents.

Among the amenities built for The Villages using the CDD funds was the Spanish Springs Town Square. The same firm that worked on Universal Studios designed the square, which opened in the spring of 1994. Spanish Springs gave residents a place to gather and brought The Villages one step closer to becoming the all-inclusive community dreamed of by Schwartz.

With roads, clubhouses, golf courses and other amenities already in place, people were eager to buy and build in The Villages. Sales climbed. By 2001, The Villages grew by an average of 10 new residents a day. The community had three churches, 16 restaurants, 13 pools, 28 tennis courts and a myriad of championship and executive golf courses. Home prices ranged from $65,000 to $650,000, and more than 27,000 people called The Villages home.

The Villages also had its own media outlets – smartly controlled by the community's developers: The Villages Daily Sun newspaper, with a circulation of 19,500; Village News Network television station; and a radio station, WVLG 640 AM.

The Villages Regional Medical Center opened its doors in 2002, and by the time The Villages founder, Harold Schwartz died in 2003, the community spread across three counties and had more than 35,000 residents. Schwartz's ashes are interred in the base of the statue depicting him at Spanish Springs Town Square:

That year The Villages was number 25 on Builder Magazine's Top 100 List and reported $668 million in gross revenue, a 44 percent increase from the year before.

As usual, profits from the development were being put back into the project. As well as golf courses and roads, in 2004

The Department of Veterans Affairs accepted Gary Morse's offer to build a veterans clinic in Sumter County.

It seemed like growth and prosperity for The Villages couldn't be stopped. According to construction contractors in 2004, homeowners were moving into their new homes in as little as 90 days after purchasing their lot. To keep up with demand, more than 100,000 yards of material were being moved each day, six days a week.

Harkening back to the previous booms of the 1920s and 50s, savvy promotion was driving sales. The Villages was advertised on television "up North" during the Gridiron Classic football games (played at the community's polo stadium), and during other bowl games. The Villages also advertised during The Disney Classic golf tournaments, which were played on The Villages courses, as well as many other nationally televised golf tournaments.

A golf lifestyle had long been a part of The Villages. By 2005 it had 18 executive courses and 7 championship courses, with the most recent championship courses being designed by Nancy Lopez and another by Arnold Palmer. Villagers not only cruised the courses in their golf carts, but also drove them to the store and to the town squares. That year The Villages also had the honor of holding the world's longest golf cart parade.

Along with the golf courses and cart paths, in 2005, The Villages amenities tally stacked up to: more than 30 tennis courts, 26 pools; 5 softballs fields; bowling centers; 74 shuffleboard courts;

72 bocce ball courts; 56 pickleball courts; 57 billiards tables and 53 horseshoe pits. Plus, The Villages had two town squares, a wellness center, a performing arts center, 12 recreation centers (and clubs to keep them full), a polo stadium and a herd of buffalo.

By 2007 The Villages was one of the largest retirement communities in the U.S., boasting more than 67,000 residents. It had added six more golf courses and the number of pools almost doubled. Also, as reported by the Sarasota Harold Tribune, residents of The Villages had clubs for "just about any legal activity known to man."

Census reports in 2008 ranked The Villages as one of the fastest-growing micropolitan areas in the nation. Population reached 75,000 residents in 38,000 homes, and The Villages of Lake Sumter ranked among the state's top private companies. The Villages crossed over the 100,000 people mark in 2012.

Around 2013 The Villages became classified as a metropolitan area instead of a micropolitan area, and US Census Bureau figures released in 2014 ranked The Villages as the nation's fastest growing metropolitan area.

From 2012 to 2013 The Villages grew 5.2 percent, gaining more than 5,300 new people. Between 2013 and 2014, The Villages population grew another 5.4%, making it the fastest growing metropolitan area in the country for the second year in a row.

Passing The Torch

Gary Morse passed away at the age of 77 in October of 2014. After his passing, tributes poured in from local, state, and national political leaders including Jeb Bush, Marco Rubio, and then Florida Governor Rick Scott who wrote:

> *"Gary was a champion of Florida innovation. When molding The Villages into the one-of-a-kind community it is today, Gary demonstrated what makes our state so great – the idea that anyone can make a positive, lasting impact in the lives of generations to come. Gary's boldness and entrepreneurial spirit is known internationally and helped define Florida as the place where anything is possible. Ann and I send our condolences to Renee, the Morse family and the entire community of The Villages today."*

His kids Mark Morse, Jennifer Parr, and Tracy Morse, who have long worked alongside him in the development of the community, vowed to keep his dreams for the future of the community alive.

3

THE VILLAGES TODAY

A nd since Gary Morse's passing, they have done just that!

In 2021, the U.S. Census Bureau named it the fastest growing metropolitan area in the country between the 2010 and 2020 Census, growing 39% from about 93,000 people to about 130,000 people.

For as long as The Villages has been around, there's always been a fear among some residents that the developers would one day sell out to some big conglomerate and things would go downhill. After all, these things often happen when there is a changing of the guard. But the development team now in place has said repeatedly that they are here to stay, and their actions have backed up those words.

Members of the developers family hold active roles in almost every facet of the business. From the development team itself, to the marketing department, the sales and leasing division, the design team, the entertainment division, and more, you don't have to look far to find someone related either by blood or by marriage to the community's leadership.

In earlier editions of this book I would mention the looming "build-out" or completion of the community, as The Villages was simply running out of land to build on. The developers themselves would even allude to the end of construction in their annual addresses and in marketing materials.

In a video put out in the summer of 2015 as they were opening up the Village of Pine Ridge, Director of Sales Jennifer Parr stated:

"At long last, the moment we've all been anticipating, the grand opening of our final phase of new homes, the Village of Pine Ridge and the Village of Pine Hills."

But in the last few years, things have definitely changed. They've acquired a lot more land, and instead of "build-out" it's all about growth, expansion, and as the developers put it, "Continuing the Dream".

In the first installment of their "Continuing the Dream" video series, you'll meet the current developers, siblings Mark, Jennifer, and Tracy, and get a look at their plans for the future of The Villages:

youtu.be/WqoFU6psa_s

Carts at Lake Sumter Landing

New Home Sales

The Villages has held the #1 spot in the country for new home sales on a pretty consistent basis, but in 2016 they were edged out by Irvine Ranch out in California.

According to John Burns Real Estate Consulting, in 2017 The Villages regained the top spot with 2,231 new home sales, and they posted 2,134 new home sales in 2018, 2,429 new home sales in 2019, and 2,452 new home sales in 2020.

You can find The Villages new home sales stats dating back almost two decades at:

insidethebubble.net/new-home-sales/

There is another Florida community, Lakewood Ranch, nipping at The Villages heels the last few years, but it is a multi-generational (all ages) community. Lakewood Ranch posted 2,149 new home sales in 2020.

But the fact that The Villages has and continues to sell as many new homes as it does while being an age restricted community, is very remarkable. Which leads me to a question I am asked more and more these days...

Is The Villages *Still* a 55+ Community?

Read enough forum posts, articles, or news reports about The Villages and one thing that might catch your attention is that there seem to be more and more residents younger than 55.

Why is that, and how can it be in what is technically a 55+ community?

The law governing 55+ communities states that at least 80% of the homes must be occupied by someone older than 55 for a community to have the 55+ designation. The 20% leeway is there to allow for special circumstances.

For example let's say a husband and wife move to The Villages. He is 55 and she is 50. If he passes away before she turns 55, she will still be allowed to live there because of this 20% leeway.

Extend this scenario beyond a spouse passing away, and consider that more and more young people in their 20's and 30's are living at home with mom and dad. Whether they've gone through a divorce, a rough stretch of unemployment, have health issues, or maybe they're actually taking care of their parents or in some cases grandparents who have health issues of their own or need special care.

While the rules state that no one under 19 may live in a home in The Villages permanently, there's nothing against anyone older than 19 doing so.

Another way that residents under 55 slip through is due to a lack of enforcement. To my knowledge The Villages can and does enforce the rules on the sales that occur through their offices, but the same scrutiny can be lacking on outside resales and in particular, rentals.

The houses, amenities, and way of life here in The Villages are certainly meant to attract a 55+ crowd, but as you can see, there are certain barriers to ensuring that it is only 55+.

One place you'll hear more and more about in the next few years is called Middleton by The Villages. Middleton will offer homes, restaurants, shopping, recreation, schools, and other amenities designed specifically for families of those who work in The Villages in some capacity, no matter their age.

So to circle back to the question posed at the beginning of this section, yes, The Villages is still predominantly a 55+ community, but you might start to see some younger and younger faces around town.

The Villages South of State Road 44

In early 2016 The Villages announced the development of approximately 3,000 more homes in the Village of Fenney, to be located about 4 miles south of what was then The Villages.

When first announced, it was said that even though Fenney would not be golf cart accessible from The Villages, residents of Fenney would enjoy the same privileges and use of facilities that all other residents of The Villages have.

Things changed quickly though after that first announcement, and since then The Villages has announced the acquisition of enough land to essentially double the size of the community, projecting that it will take 20-30 years for everything to be built.

The first residents began moving into this new area south of 44 in 2017, and several more neighborhoods, recreation centers, and other amenities have opened in this new area, as you'll read about later in the book.

The first bridges over State Road 44 and the Florida Turnpike for carts, cyclists, and pedestrians are now in place, with more to follow.

No doubt it is a very exciting time in The Villages, particularly for those moving into all of the new areas. But moving to the southern portion of The Villages where all of this is happening currently results in a trade-off.

On one hand, residents are getting the latest and greatest amenities. No one can argue that the recreation centers and other amenities being built down here aren't bigger and better than what exists in the rest of the community.

But it will take some time before there are enough grocery stores, restaurants, and other amenities to satisfy everyone. Residents in the new areas will also be dealing with construction traffic for many years to come. There is a limestone quarry to the south and west of all of this new development, and some Village of Fenney residents have complained about blasting occurring at the quarry occasionally rattling their windows.

Something else you hear people talk about is the presence of Coleman Federal Prison, also just a couple miles away from homes in The Villages, which was once home to Boston crime boss James "Whitey" Bulger. If you Google "Coleman Federal Prison" you can read more about the prison and see an interesting list of other inmates that have been there.

Maybe these things don't bother or matter to you. To many people, they don't. But I see posts on resident message boards and forums all the time with people saying things like "my salesperson never told me about that!" so this is me telling you to do your research and necessary due diligence.

Navigating the Pandemic

The Covid-19 pandemic threw everyone for a loop, The Villages included. But compared to a lot of places, the community fared pretty well. You'll learn more about how The Villages' special purpose government works later in the book, but the main thing to know is it eliminates a lot of red tape, and allows the developer and local government (a.k.a. "The District") to make decisions and act quickly to protect residents when necessary, evidence of which was on full display in 2020-2021.

Love it or hate it, the developer's political connections (which you'll also learn about later in the book) likely also benefitted residents throughout the pandemic, as The Villages was able to quickly secure the testing (drive-thru covid testing in your golf cart anyone?), medical resources, and eventually vaccines, needed to fight the virus.

The governor and other high level officials visited multiple times, and The Villages pandemic response was cited in articles by publications like The New York Times, The Wall Street Journal, and many others.

From March 2020 to March 2021, approximately 3% of residents ended up contracting Covid-19. Unfortunately some of them passed away, but because The Villages is spread across three counties, each with different methods and means of reporting, I can't say for sure how many Villages residents died. Perhaps one day that information will be available for those who are curious.

However, I documented all of the major developments throughout the pandemic, from my first post on March 13, 2020 to the present day at:

insidethebubble.net/coronavirus/

I encourage you to check out that page and scroll down to the March 13, 2020 entry and many of the entries that followed. It will give you a good understanding of how things went here during this crazy time.

4

WHY HAS THE VILLAGES BEEN SO SUCCESSFUL?

Occasionally I spend time with developers across the country who bring me in to pick my brain about The Villages. The main thing they want to know is some variation of the question:

"Why has The Villages been so successful?"

If you think of the popular real estate mantra "Location, Location, Location" and take into account that The Villages started essentially in the middle of nowhere, then you could probably rattle off 50 communities that should be more successful than The Villages.

Yet, they're not. So what's the secret ingredient?

Of course there are several things, and I'm going to leave out the usual suspects like more golf courses than you can shake a club at, more than 3,000 clubs and organized groups, golf cart accessible restaurants, shopping, healthcare and so on, even though all of those things are important.

They've definitely given people what they want and have most of the basics down pat. But those are readily apparent ingredients to The Villages' success that anyone can see.

Here I want to share a few of the less obvious answers I usually give when I get this question.

A Story That Spreads Easily

Lake Sumter Landing Boardwalk

The Villages story is easy to spread. When most people visit Florida looking for a place to retire they'll likely visit a bunch of communities but from experience I can tell you after you see a handful of them, for the most part they tend to run together.

You'll see beautiful houses, great golf courses, clubhouses and other amenities in all of them, but there's usually very little that stands out as unique.

The Villages has that uniqueness.

Part of it is the sheer size and amount of things available. This makes it stand out in people's minds when discussing various communities. Part of it is the idea of "free golf for life", that's a unique story that makes it easy to go home and tell friends about!

Also, because of their success, The Villages gets a lot of press, both good and bad. Every time a major Republican politician (or the President himself) visits to give a speech, campaign for election, or do a book signing in The Villages and it gets picked up by major news outlets across the country, more people hear about this place called The Villages.

When a golf cart video goes viral and racks up 4,000,000+ views like one CBS Morning Show segment did a few years ago, more people hear about The Villages. You can't buy that kind of marketing and if you could, you probably couldn't afford it!

Even the bad press and publicity The Villages sometimes receives helps to further spread The Villages name and story. What's the saying? "There's no such thing as bad publicity?"

The Villages has done a great job implementing "the uniqueness factor" into their marketing as well, going all the way back to when Harold Schwartz used to have prospective buyers picked up at the airport in a limo. You think those people went home and told their friends about that unique experience? You bet they did.

Today the sheer size of the community and the fact that it is still growing and evolving to meet the needs of future retirees is part of that unique story.

Longevity

It's easy to look at the success of The Villages and assume it came overnight. In reality, The Villages is anything but an overnight success.

A few chapters ago we discussed how The Villages began as a struggling mobile home park and survived through a handful of recessions, real estate downturns, and now, even a global pandemic.

But they've managed to stick it out through thick and thin, and even though their "thin" times were not as bad as that of many others, you have to give them credit for staying the course.

It's a Family Affair

When you look at the size of The Villages and the amount of home sales and revenue they generate each year, without knowing the make-up of the organization and the history, an outsider could easily assume that a giant publicly traded corporation is running the show.

Yet that's not the case. It's basically one family at the wheel.

Now of course they have lots of help…I'm not trying to discount the efforts of all those outside the family who make The Villages a success. What I mean here is that success has been a result of the focused leadership of three generations of one family.

Make no doubt about it, this is their baby. They have skin in the game. It's their family name on the line every day.

I think we'd all agree you're going to put a little more effort into something when it's your family legacy behind it, rather than just some company you collect a paycheck from.

The advantage of this is that every decision, right or wrong, is made in their vision. And because of that, they've been able to create an exemplary community. Oftentimes what happens when you take a company by committee...a building by committee...a community by committee...you don't get a fantastic product.

You don't get an exemplary product or outcome.

You get what you often get through committee which is a little bit of bureaucracy...and I dare say a little bit of mediocrity.

Over on the right, sales and marketing wants the community to have certain amenities or build certain types of homes because it's what people want. But over on the left, the finance guys who need to make their numbers for the quarter say no, we're going to do these kinds of amenities and build these types of houses. Unfortunately I see this type of thinking go on in the development of so many other communities.

It's tough to create a big success when those kinds of forces are working against each other, but thankfully, The Villages doesn't seem to have those problems. But, that's not to say the place is perfect, no place is, as you'll read about in the next chapter.

5
CRITICISM: BOOKS, ARTICLES, AND DOCUMENTARIES

Over the years there have been a handful of books, articles, and documentaries, that paint a picture of The Villages as some sort of booze and drug fueled 24-hour party town.

Presenting a retirement community in this manner probably does a lot to help sell books, get traffic to a website, or sell movie tickets, but it just couldn't be any further from the truth.

If you read these books and articles or watch these documentaries and are hoping that's what you'll really find here, I'm sorry to be the bearer of bad news. You are going to be sorely disappointed! I've been writing about The Villages for well over a decade now, and I've never had one person tell me they came and checked it out but it was just "too wild and crazy" for them.

But at the same time, I feel it's important to put these things on your radar because you will likely hear about them at some point in your journey.

Book: *Leisureville: Adventures in a World Without Children*

While not entirely about The Villages, Leisureville, published in 2008, explores the topic of "age-segregated retirement", something that the book's author Andrew Blechman makes clear he is not a fan of.

After neighbors in his New England town retire to The Villages, Mr. Blechman sets off to learn what they find so appealing about the concept of living in a 55+ community.

While the book garnered a lot of acclaim from critics, it received mostly criticism from residents, who felt that many of the characters were made up or exaggerated to help the book garner more attention. One example is a character named Chet, a self-proclaimed lady-killer nicknamed "Mr. Midnight". Let's just say his exploits in the book are not PG rated.

How much of the experiences and characters described are true and how much are exaggerations, I don't think anyone other than the author can truly say. But I seriously doubt you'll ever meet "Chet" and you especially won't be doing it at his favorite pick-up spot, Katie Belle's, as it closed for good in 2020.

Article: *Romance and STD's: Inside Florida's Wild Retirees Getaway*

One question I get quite often goes something like "I heard The Villages has the highest rate of Sexually Transmitted Diseases in the country! Is that really true?"

No, as I'm about to prove to you it is absolutely not true. But some readers are very concerned about it:

> *"Ryan – One of my biggest concerns is that every time I mention The Villages to anyone I am told 'do you know that The Villages have the highest rate of STD's in the United States?' Let me share with you that it totally disgusts me regarding the statement! But now my question is why do people say this all the time? Is it true?"*

From another reader:

> *"Ryan – ... so many people "back home" bring a topic to our attention when we mention our interest in moving there. Apparently, The Villages has been noted as having (one of) the highest rates of STD in the country!! Although we would not plan to participate in furthering this statistic, we are certainly curious about the validity of this statistic and why. It doesn't seem to be reflective of the impression that The Villages tries to make on creating a friendly (and healthy) environment for retiring Americans."*

One article responsible for starting this rumor is titled "Romance and STD's: Inside Florida's wild retirees getaway" by Stefanie Cohen published in January 25, 2009 on the website of the New York Post. The book *Leisureville* is mentioned and was likely the inspiration for the article, which was published just a few months after the book.

You can read the article at this link: nypost.com/2009/01/25/retire-to-the-bedroom/

An excerpt:

> *"Welcome to ground zero for geriatrics who are seriously getting it on. It's a Thursday night at one of a half-dozen hot spots at the 20,000-acre Central Florida complex called The Villages, the largest gated retirement community in America – and one of the most popular destinations for New Yorkers in their golden years – where the female-to-male ratio runs 10 to 1. It's a widower's paradise, and the word on the street is that there's a big black market for Viagra."*

First of all, the statistic of a female-to-male ratio of "10 to 1" should tip you off that this article is not dealing in reality. Keep in mind that this is from the New York Post, which has been criticized numerous times for "sensationalism".

To discover the truth about the STD rumor you can visit the Florida Department of Health website and see the stats for yourself. If you do that, you'll learn that Sumter County (the county in which most of The Villages sits) has the lowest rate of STD's in the entire state of Florida. I just verified this again on October 30, 2021 before publishing this update to the book.

But no matter what I or the actual numbers say, word about this stuff really "gets around" (pun intended) because it's far from what people expect to hear about life in a retirement community. It makes for fun pub or golf course banter among buddies.

Now, just because the STD rumors are untrue, I'm not saying that *all* of the stories you may hear aren't true. There *have* been some real (and true) doozies in the past.

For instance, back in 2014 a 68-year old resident was arrested along with her 49-year old lover for having sex at the pavilion at Lake Sumter Landing. Another couple that same year was arrested for having sex on an electrical utility box at 8:42 in the morning in full view of the public.

But keep in mind, stories like these are the exception, not the rule.

Some Kind of Heaven

In January 2021, an 81-minute film titled *Some Kind of Heaven*, directed by Lance Oppenheim, was released in selected theaters and on demand. The film was also an Official Selection of the 2020 Sundance Film Festival.

Here's the summary that appeared on IMDB and on the director's website:

> *"Behind the gates of a palm tree-lined fantasyland, four residents of America's largest retirement community, The Villages, FL, strive to find happiness and meaning."*

In an article on the Sundance blog, the director said this about why he made the film:

> *"I was fascinated that hundreds of thousands of people were moving from across the country to live in this kind of isolated Truman Show–like bubble town, and I wanted to see what that was like for myself."*

I encourage you to watch the film, in large part due to the stunning videography. You really get a great visual of how gorgeous The Villages is. But please keep in mind that much like the books and articles we've highlighted so far in this chapter, *Some Kind of Heaven* also leaned more towards the "sensational" rather than the "reality".

One of the four main characters is not even a resident, rather, an octogenarian living out of his van, taking showers at the neighborhood pools, and trying to find a rich widow to support him. Another character who has been married to his wife for 47 years is dealing with a drug problem. You feel sympathetic towards him, and the wife who must deal with his antics, but they're hardly "typical" residents.

Speak with 99.9% of residents and they would say that they don't have any neighbors like these characters in the film.

That said, sometimes people forget just how big this community is. 130,000+ people is not a small community by any stretch of the imagination. Take just about any other city/town/community in the country of that size and I'm sure you will find that sex, drugs, and alcohol are all available in certain quantities there too.

I think it just interests people more because these aren't the kinds of activities you'd expect to hear retirees partaking in, even if it's just a small percentage of the population. Everyone thinks a retirement community should be all "lemonade" and "shuffle board". But these are real people you're talking about. To my knowledge they are built and wired up the same way as people everywhere else.

At the time of this writing *Some Kind of Heaven* is available to stream on Hulu, or to rent or buy from Amazon Prime Video.

The Bubble

The Bubble, not to be confused with a handful of other films with the same title (including one about another Florida community, Celebration) is another documentary about The Villages from 2021.

Written and directed by Valerie Blankenbyl, The Bubble has not been released in the U.S. as of this writing, but I was able to see it when it was screened at the 2021 Sarasota Film Festival.

From the film's description:

> "In the "Villages" (the world's largest retirement community) there are not only supermarkets, but also bars and restaurants. From belly dancing to synchronized swimming, everything that a pensioner's heart desires is offered. But what appears to be the fulfillment of the American dream at first glance, cracks upon closer inspection. After all, maintaining this bubble not only has a price for its inhabitants, but also for the world around them."

Where *Some Kind of Heaven* focused more on the lives of a handful of characters, *The Bubble* focused more on the concept of The Villages, and the impacts it has on the people, the economy, and the environment both inside and outside the community.

Like *Some Kind of Heaven*, *The Bubble* is definitely not a commercial for The Villages, so if that's all you're interested in, you'll be disappointed. The filmmakers make a point several times throughout *The Bubble* to point out that they were not exactly welcomed with open arms by the developer.

A few of the problems the film sheds light on include political divisiveness, control of the developer, environmental concerns like excessive water use and sinkholes, as well as the seemingly endless growth the community is experiencing. Most of these topics are not news to residents or people who have done even a little bit of research about the community.

Much like *Some Kind of Heaven*, I enjoyed *The Bubble* for the videography. Maybe it's just me, but I just think it's really neat to see The Villages on the "big screen".

As a new or prospective resident, I know it can be a pain to have "people back home" bring up these rumors, or articles and movies, and possibly poke fun at your decision about where to retire.

Try not to let it get to you. Just remember that it could be ignorance or it could be jealousy, because we as humans have a habit of if we can't have something or don't like something, we don't want anybody else to have it or like it either.

6

GETTING TO REALLY KNOW THE VILLAGES

In this chapter I've listed websites and other sources of information that will help you get to know The Villages even better.

To save you time, each week I go through each and every resource mentioned here and highlight the most interesting news and information from that week in my Saturday morning email newsletter. You can learn more and sign-up here (it's free):

insidethebubble.net/this-week/

The Villages Daily Sun

One thing you will hear pretty consistently is that the developer-owned The Villages Daily Sun newspaper does not cover any news that could be detrimental to the development or the developer. What you get with the Daily Sun are the "feel good" stories, which will still give you some good information on what life is like in The Villages, but it doesn't give you any of the not so good news that sometimes happens.

thevillagesdailysun.com

The Villages Magazine

The Villages also puts out a monthly magazine with light-hearted articles and stories about the people and things you'll encounter during every day life in The Villages. You can pick up a copy at several locations throughout The Villages, or read the digital edition online.

thevillagesdailysun.com/magazine/

Villages-News.com

Another website on the scene worth mentioning is Villages-News.com, run by a former editor of The Villages Daily Sun. They're doing a great job covering what's really going on in The Villages.

Villages-News.com

Talk of The Villages

At this website, which is a forum for residents and prospective residents of The Villages, you can essentially "spy" on the residents...and of course I don't mean "spy" on them in the stalker type sense...but you can sit back and listen to their conversations, pick their brains if you have questions, and see what everyday life in The Villages is like.

talkofthevillages.com

The Villages Best YouTube Channels

If video is your preferred way to consume content and you are trying to learn more about The Villages, you are in luck!

There are a handful of "YouTubers" that call The Villages home who are putting out great content on a regular basis. These include The Villages Newcomers, Skip Smith, Rusty Nelson, Gold Wingnut, Pryde of The Villages, Exploring The Villages Florida, and several more.

For a complete list of the YouTube channels about The Villages that I follow, visit:

insidethebubble.net/the-villages-best-youtube-channels/

7
COME FOR A VISIT

You can read articles and books or watch movies and video on YouTube all you want, but the best way to separate fact from fiction is to come see it for yourself.

Fortunately, The Villages makes this easy for anyone to do.

They offer a "visitation" program called Lifestyle Preview Program where you can come visit, stay in one of the homes here, and really experience what it's like to live in The Villages. While it's not free, the rates are much better than getting a local hotel room, even a budget hotel at that.

You can check current rates and schedule your visit at:

thevillages.com/lifestyle-preview-plan

The Lifestyle Preview allows prospective residents the opportunity to come live like a Villager for anywhere from 4 to 7 nights. The Villages will put you up in one of their fully-furnished homes which will have everything you'd expect from a typical vacation rental and even includes your very own golf cart and bicycles for getting around while you are here.

Christmastime at Brownwood

The Villages will also set you up with a salesperson to give you the nickel tour, but it's far from a timeshare pitch, the place pretty much sells itself.

At the time of this writing the rates are January $179; February and March $199; April $149; May-September $99; and October-December $149. These prices are obviously subject to change without notice.

Some people visiting don't even bother to rent a car. If you fly directly into Orlando International Airport, you can just hop one of the airport shuttles that I'll tell you about in Chapter 9, which will bring you right to The Villages.

Personally though, I'd recommend renting a car because that will allow you to cover a lot more ground while you're checking out the areas in and around The Villages.

What Else Is Included?

When you check-in you'll receive an ID card and gate pass which will allow you access to all the amenities residents get to enjoy everyday. Though some of the other free benefits change from time-to-time, the last time I checked you got one round of championship golf and one round of executive course golf per person, two theater tickets, and a book with coupons and discounts for use at select restaurants and retailers.

There has been a noticeable reduction in the amount of freebies given in recent years because the community seems to sell itself pretty well. Many years ago The Villages used to pick up preview guests in a stretch limo at the airport! Sadly, those days are gone now.

What To Bring?

As I mentioned, the place where you'll be staying will have just about everything you'd need. Just pack like you would normally for a vacation. You can either bring your golf clubs or rent a set when you get here. Don't forget to bring along your checkbook, in case you fall in love and find a home you have to have.

The Villages Lifestyle Preview is something you should definitely take advantage of. The price is right, and it includes some decent perks. There's really no better way to experience what life is like in The Villages.

8
FINDING A RENTAL

Though I advise you to take advantage of the Lifestyle Preview Program offered by The Villages, sometimes its not enough time to get a good feel for what it might be like living here year round. In that case, you might want to rent a house and check out The Villages for a little while longer.

When is the best time to rent?

The time from November through April is the busiest time of the year in The Villages. This means a couple of things. For one, it makes it much harder to find a rental. It also means that restaurants, golf courses, and everything else are much more crowded than during the summer and fall.

But, if you plan to live in The Villages full-time in the future, its good to get a sense of just what "crowded" means. It may not seem crowded to you. I've heard from people that couldn't believe how bad it was, and I've heard from others who didn't think it was that bad.

So, bottom line, if you want the best selection and prices, rent from June-October. If you want the best idea of what the busy season is like, rent during the busy season. I know that many of my readers have made it a point to rent during BOTH seasons, just to be sure.

How much does it cost to rent a home in The Villages?

As you can imagine the price of rentals will vary, depending on the season. Basic supply and demand economics at work. Other things that are common sense but you should keep in mind is that the bigger the home and newer it is, the more you'll likely pay. Location is also a major factor in the rent. In general, the more centrally located the home is, or immediately near the town squares, the more you can expect to pay.

Because prices vary so much based on location and time of year, it would be difficult for me to give you price ranges for each home type you'll encounter in The Villages. But just to show you how much rates can fluctuate throughout the year, one home I found (a 3/2 Designer in Lake Deaton) had a high rate of $4,300/month in March and a low rate of $1,750/month in July.

Where should you rent?

As you probably know by now, The Villages is a huge place comprised of a lot of individual neighborhoods.

This can make it that much harder to choose a rental. You might see a house you like that seems to fit all of your needs but if it's far away from the places you'll spend most of your time, like certain golf courses and the town squares, and it can be a pain traveling to and from over long distances, especially in a golf cart.

If you can, try to find a rental that's centrally located. But if you have no preference on golf courses or between the town squares, then it may not really matter. Go with the best home you can find.

Finding a Rental

As you can see by the list that follows, there are A LOT of places to look for rentals. Don't focus your search on any one website. Be sure to explore rentals available on several of them.

Also, it's important to note that some sites show rentals where the owner is representing themselves (for rent by owner), and others are advertised and managed by local real estate agents.

The Villages Hometown Property Management – This is the developer's rental division, so you'll usually find a wide selection of rentals to choose from here.

thevillageshpm.com

VRBO – Vacation Rentals By Owner is a national rental website where homeowners pay a fee to make their rental listings available to potential short and long-term tenants. At the time of this writing they show more than 700 rentals available in The Villages.

vrbo.com/vacation-rentals/usa/florida/central-disney-orlando/the-villages

VillagersHomes4Rent.com – Started by Villages resident Don Crosby, and now managed and run by his daughter Judy VillagersHomes4Rent.com has more than 1,200 rentals listed on their site. This is not a website for full-service rentals. Private homeowners simply pay a fee to have their home and contact information listed on the site.

villagershomes4rent.com

VillagesforRent.com – This site is run by Couture Properties, LLC, offering full-service management for owners of the homes that are listed for rent.

villagesforrent.com

Our Villages Rental – Our Villages Rental now has over 100 homes on the site and offers some great features that make searching for a rental even easier. You can search availability for specific dates, which is really helpful for those looking for a week or two week rental. Large home photos make it easy to find the perfect rental home!

ourvillagesrental.com

Rent From a Villager – Launched in 2021, Rent From a Villager is another site that allows you to connect with owners directly to discuss details and arrangements for your possible rental. They don't charge any booking, service, or convenience fees for using the site.

rentfromavillager.com/rent

You might also want to do your own web search to see if you can dig up any other results for "The Villages Florida rentals".

Apartment Rentals

In 2020, the first residents moved into The Villages' first rental apartments, The Lofts at Brownwood.

The Lofts at Brownwood offers 265 one, two, and three bedroom apartments, with rental rates starting at $1,460 per month at the time of this writing. Residents of The Lofts must also pay the $164/month amenities fee, just like single family homeowners in The Villages, and by doing so, they get use of the same amenities as other residents.

thevillages.com/thelofts

The Villages has signaled a desire to put apartments in Spanish Springs, they've said the new family neighborhood you'll read about later in the book, Middleton, will have them, and I think odds are good we'll see some apartments at Eastport, the new lifestyle center in the new/future area of The Villages, so one way or another, more apartments will be popping up in The Villages in the coming years.

9

GETTING AROUND THE VILLAGES

Whether you come initially for a lifestyle preview visit or decide to rent a home for a little while, you could probably use a little help getting around. Here are some helpful resources.

The Villages App

The official mobile app from The Villages provides real-time navigation, weather and event information in the palm of your hand.

According to their website, "The Villages® App is your take-anywhere guide to Florida's Friendliest Hometown, equipped with directions for traveling by multi-modal golf car path and traditional roadways."

thevillages.com/app/

. . .

Villages GPS App

Villages GPS (which is not affiliated with the developer of The Villages) is billed as "the ultimate app for The Villages, FL."

Villages GPS is an app available from the Apple App Store or Google Play store that lives on your iPhone, iPad or Android device.

With the app, you now have a map in your phone of all the town squares, golf courses, recreation centers, and neighborhoods within The Villages.

villagesgps.com

Navigating The Villages Roundabouts

One thing that throws some first time visitors to The Villages off are the roundabouts.

Roundabouts are very prevalent in The Villages. They serve multiple purposes such as keeping traffic flowing in an orderly fashion and increasing driver safety by preventing the possibility of T-bone collisions. However, there is a good possibility that some residents have never encountered a roundabout.

In most cases, a roundabout is a circular intersection where vehicles travel in a counter-clockwise motion, generally in one or two lanes, around a central island. The most common roundabouts are four-way intersections, but they can contain even more roads in some instances.

Roundabouts are easiest to navigate when you know where you intend to exit them. Knowing where you would like to end up can be tremendously helpful when navigating your entry into the roundabout.

Perhaps the easiest way to travel through a roundabout is if you intend to make a right turn. In this instance, you should enter the roundabout in the right lane. This will take you into the outside lane of the roundabout and enable you to exit the roundabout at the next street.

If you intend to travel through the roundabout and continue straight ahead, it can be appropriate to use either lane to enter and travel through the roundabout. The only concern in this case is that you should make sure you stay in the same lane throughout and also be sure to use your turn signal when you are ready to exit. If you are exiting from the inside lane, be careful that there isn't a vehicle in the outside lane that intends to keep circling. Not everyone is aware of this guideline, so be careful in these situations.

If you are planning on using a roundabout to make a left turn or a full-circle U-turn, you will want to enter the roundabout in the left lane. You should stay in the inside lane until you are ready to exit. Once again, it is important to use your turn signal when exiting and make sure that you are not going to be hit by someone ignoring proper roundabout procedure.

Approaching Roundabouts

As you approach a roundabout, you should slow down in order to yield to any traffic that is already in the roundabout as they have the right-of-way. When you pull up to the roundabout entrance, wait for a gap in traffic that will allow you to enter in a safe manner.

Near the roundabout entrance, you will likely see a road sign that will display a map of the possible exit streets. These guide signs also specify which lane you should be in to properly proceed to your desired exit.

It is a good general rule that if you expect to exit at or before the halfway point in the roundabout, you should enter in the right lane. If you expect to exit after the halfway point of the roundabout, you should enter it in the left lane.

General Roundabout Guidelines

In order to maintain the safety of everyone using the roundabout, you should make sure to avoid changing lanes or passing other vehicles in the roundabout. You should also make every effort to avoid stopping in the roundabout, unless it is to avoid a collision.

It is also a good idea to heighten your awareness of surrounding vehicles while traveling through a roundabout. Larger vehicles may have a more difficult time navigating through roundabouts, and there is always the possibility of a driver who simply neglects to follow the rules. You should be cautious to keep your distance from either of these situations.

The roundabouts in The Villages do a great job of both increasing the flow of traffic and reducing the possibility of dangerous collisions. However, as you can see, there are quite a few rules and guidelines that go along with their proper usage. It is easy to see how someone who is unfamiliar with these rules could cause an accident. Make sure that you are fully aware of how to properly proceed through a roundabout, so that we all can arrive safely to our next destination.

Getting To and From the Airport

People come to The Villages from all over the world, which means that there is a steady stream of travelers going back and forth between The Villages and Orlando International Airport. There are a couple of ways to get here.

Driving Yourself

The easiest way to get to and from the airport might be to drive yourself. If you are visiting The Villages for the first time, you can rent a car from any of the rental car companies located right in the airport. The drive is not complicated and should take you around 60-70 minutes.

If, like so many first time visitors, you are taking advantage of the Lifestyle Preview Plan, the address you'll want to program into your car's GPS or your favorite navigation app on your phone is 2705 West Torch Lake Drive, The Villages, FL 32163. That's the address of the Brownwood Paddock Square Sales and Information Center where you'll check in for your stay.

Coming out of the airport's North exit you will head west on Florida 528, then get on the Florida Turnpike heading North. Stay on that for just over 50 miles, take exit 304 for Wildwood, and follow your phone or car's navigation from there.

But, if you'd rather not drive, there are other options available.

Workman Transportation

Workman Transportation (previously known as The Villages Transportation) offers non-stop transportation to and from Orlando International Airport (OIA), thirteen times per day, seven days per week. The service picks up at Lake Sumter Landing and Brownwood Paddock Square on a regular schedule that is published on their website. They also offer return trips that pick up at terminals A14-15 and B14-15 below the baggage claim.

Workman Transportation charges $35 per passenger each way if you book online, or $40 if you book over the phone. They will also pick you up from or drop you off at your house for an additional $15 charge.

In addition to the OIA shuttle service, they also offer a private car service that will take you to OIA, Orlando-Sanford Airport, and Port Canaveral (where several cruise lines are based). Rates are posted on their website.

workmantransportation.com

(352) 259-9398

Village Airport Van

If you've spent any amount of time in The Villages, there's a good chance that you've seen the Village Airport Van's signature white vans with yellow stripes. They offer a door-to-door shared ride service that allows Villagers to be picked up from their homes and taken directly to the airport. Because this is a shared ride service, there may be multiple stops on your ride, but they try to keep it to as few stops as possible.

Village Airport Van provides service to/from Orlando International Airport (MCO) and Orlando/Sanford (SFB). Their rates start at $40 per passenger, but they offer discounts for parties of 3 or more. One neat benefit, if you ever have any active duty military friends or relatives visiting you once you move to The Villages, they ride for free!

villageairportvan.com

352-241-4000

IT'S A GOLF CART LIFE

Golf carts are a way of life for most Villagers. Even non-golfers find it more convenient to hop in their golf cart to get around The Villages than in their cars. It's easier to park a golf cart too, as most of the shopping centers, entertainment venues, town squares and medical facilities are considered "golf cart approved" or "accessible".

As you can imagine, golf carts are a VERY big industry in The Villages. There are companies that sell and service carts, companies that rent carts, companies that insure carts, and even companies that provide roadside assistance for golf carts.

The best advice I can give you as far as golf art shopping is concerned is to narrow it down to a make/model you like and shop around for the best combination of price, selection, and service.

Here are a few golf cart dealers to check out.

The Villages Golf Cars has locations throughout the community including at Lake Sumter Landing, Brownwood, La Plaza Grande, and Magnolia Plaza.

thevillagesgolfcarstore.com

Streetrod Golf Cars - If you're looking to go all out and really turn heads driving through The Villages, Streetrod Golf Cars builds "Unforgettable Custom Golf Cars", and they sure are fancy!

streetrodgolfcars.com

Villages Golf Cart Man – Villages Golf Cart Man has been around almost as long as people have been buying golf carts in The Villages.

villagesgolfcartman.com

Cart World Golf Cars - Located on 441 in Lady Lake, they offer sales, service, and rentals.

cartworldgolfcars.com

Village Discount Golf Car - Offering sales, service, and rentals, they are located in the Santa Fe Crossing Plaza on CR466.

villagediscountgolfcar.com

How to Find a Golf Cart Rental

When visiting The Villages, you might want to rent a golf cart. If you are visiting on Lifestyle Preview Program, your rental will come with a golf cart.

If you need a rental for other reasons, most of the places I listed previously in this chapter also rent carts. Keep in mind that several factors go into what you will end up paying to rent a golf cart and the choices available to you.

These factors include time of year (during the busy season Jan-April many places don't have carts available), how many seats you need (2 or 4 usually), the speed of the carts, whether or not they have enclosures (tip: you definitely want enclosures), and how long you want to rent for.

Most companies rent on a weekly or monthly basis, but some rent by the day if that's what you need. Call and see what you can work out.

Golf Cart Citation Story

The story below is from someone who received a citation while driving their golf cart in The Villages and I thought it was worth sharing with you here.

Inside the Bubble

It's a great reminder that when you're in a golf cart, traffic laws still apply and they might be different than the laws you follow when in your car.

The Villages Homeowners Advocates put on monthly golf cart safety clinics the third Wednesday of every month. These clinics are held with representatives from the Sumter County Sheriff's Office. If you are unsure of the laws that govern the operation of your cart, it wouldn't hurt to attend one of these.

Anyway, here's the email I received: (Names have been removed to protect the innocent)

Recently my wife and I were going to Spanish Springs to meet another couple for dinner and a movie. Somewhere along Morse Blvd., out of the blue, I see a Deputy Sheriff on a motorcycle with his lights flashing behind me in the (Golf Cart) 'Diamond Lane'.

I pulled to a stop and the Deputy informed me that I was exceeding 20mph in my "golf cart". He gave me a slip of paper which stated that the Florida Statute 320.01 defines a golf cart as a vehicle which is NOT CAPABLE of exceeding 20 mph.

Because of this, when I exceeded 20 mph I was no longer in a golf cart but I was driving a motorized vehicle on public roads without proper registration or license. He then served me with a citation to that effect and told me it was a criminal offense.

He also said that if I produced a certified letter from a golf cart shop that the golf cart was adjusted to not exceed 20 mph the judge may let me off with just court costs. The citation had a date that I was to appear in the county court in Bushnell, FL. It also stated "Criminal Violation court appearance required".

I thought to myself – here I am enjoying one of the most talked about benefits of "Florida's Most Friendly City" on my way to a movie and I end up as a criminal.

I was very anxious so when I got home I searched the internet trying to find out how hot the water was that I was in. I went to TalkOfTheVillages and found some discussion related to my situation.

I went to the Sumter County Clerk website and found that a CLASS 2 Misdemeanor was a Criminal offense punishable with a fine of up to $500 and 6 months in the county jail.

I thought WHAT! – Morse Blvd. has a speed limit of 30mph – I was not going any speed close to the limit and I could end up fined and in jail because I was in a golf cart and not in a car. And in addition to that I will now have a CRIMINAL RECORD.

Going to Court

I appeared in court in Bushnell at 9:00 a.m. on the proper date. Misdemeanor offenses are prosecuted in Courtroom B of the court house. The Judge took time to explain in great detail how the pleading process worked and the procedure that followed each type of plea. He also said that he puts everyone on probation, usually for six months, to allow them time to pay the costs incurred. One important note stated by the judge is that he evaluates each case on its own merits, so a person *should not expect the same sentencing as any other person who committed the same violation. His questions to each person who I witnessed appearing before him, including myself, were to clarify the violation and circumstances related to it.*

When I was called to come before him, he read the charge and asked me for my plea. My plea was "No Contest" because I had no idea I was creating a criminal offense by driving the golf cart in excess of 20 mph. I now know I was wrong, but I didn't even think I was speeding since Morse Blvd. has a 30 mph speed limit.

The Judge was very pleasant and professional while carrying out his duties. He didn't fine me but told me I had court costs to pay and that he was withholding adjudication for which I am very grateful. Also, I was placed on probation until the costs were paid.

I then had some papers to sign in the courtroom. After this I went to the County Clerk's office to set up payment and find out the amounts due ($253-court costs) and then to the cashiers office to pay – cash, credit card, (no personal checks). She sent me down the street to take the probation clerk my receipt. The lady at this office had me fill out more papers of personal info. for their system and pay them $50. This could only be a money order, nothing else – no cash, no check, no credit card, only a money order. The lady in the office said I could get a money order at the Shell gas station on the corner. I walked to the gas station and gave the clerk $51.50 for the $50 money order. After I gave the lady in the *probation office the $50 money order she said the case was closed and I should get written notification within a week.*

THE GOOD

All the people at the courthouse were nice and pleasant to deal with. That includes the clerks, the deputies, and the Judge.

THE BAD

It cost $304.50 at the courthouse and approximately $125.00 for the certification of the golf cart. TOTAL $429.50

THE UGLY

At the end of the process you have a CRIMINAL RECORD.

NOTE: Before you can enter the courtroom you must be wearing long pants (no Shorts), a tucked in shirt that is buttoned up, no hat, no sunglasses, no chewing gum.

My advice – Don't exceed 20mph in a golf cart – Drive your car if you need to go faster.

Golf Cart Safety

As much fun and convenient as they are, golf carts are not without risks. Almost every year there are several golf cart related accidents involving serious injury and sometimes death here in The Villages.

The Villages Homeowners Advocates (VHA) host Free Golf Cart Safety Clinics at the Colony Recreation Center at 9:00 AM on the third Wednesday of each month.

I encourage all new cart owners to attend one of these clinics where you will learn safety tips, cart maintenance tips, and can get insurance information. Until then, you can also watch the Golf Cart Safety video they have on YouTube:

youtu.be/QcvwRmbZcFY

11
GOLF & TENNIS

Florida is considered by many to be the golf capital of the U.S. There's even a license plate proclaiming just that. But if Florida is the golf capital of the United States, The Villages is definitely the golf capital of Florida.

The Villages has more holes of golf than any other community/facility in the world and at the time of this writing in late 2021 there are 711 holes of golf in The Villages.

Executive Courses

There are now 42 Executive courses in The Villages. These mostly nine-hole courses (*Marsh View Pitch & Putt has 18 holes*) are primarily par 3's with a few par 4's and the rare par 5 sprinkled in for fun.

These courses are free for residents to play...if you live in The Villages, you're in! You'll pay no greens fees and if you want to walk the course it's free. But, there is a small fee for golf cart rental. You can also use your own cart and pay a trail fee either daily, semi-annually, or annually.

One of the newest and most exciting additions to that list is the Marsh View Pitch & Putt, a golf cart free course that features holes ranging from 40-110 yards in length. Considered a par-3 course, golfers can expect to play a quick 18-hole round in about an hour and a half.

Another fun addition not on this list because it's not an actual executive course is The Villages' very first professionally designed putting course, Fenney Putt & Play, which feature two nine-hole putting courses, lawn bowling and croquet greens, and a walking trail, all located on a very cool island in the Village of Fenney. I mention a few other new "specialty golf" locations later in this chapter.

Executive Golf Course Locations

Spanish Springs Area (North of County Road 466)

Amberwood, Briarwood, Chula Vista, De La Vista, El Diablo, El Santiago, Hawkes Bay, Hill Top, Mira Mesa, Oakleigh, Saddlebrook, Silver Lake, Walnut Grove

Lake Sumter Landing Area (Between County Road 466 and 466-A)

Bacall, Belmont, Bogart, Bonita Pass, Churchill Greens, Heron, Lowlands, Okeechobee, Pelican, Pimlico, Redfish Run, Roosevelt, Sandhill, Southern Star, Tarpon Boil, Truman, Turtle Mound, Yankee Clipper

Brownwood Area: (Between 466-A and State Road 44)

Escambia, Mangrove, Okeechobee, Palmetto, Sarasota, Sweetgum, Volusia

New and Future Areas (South of State Road 44)

Gray Fox, Loblolly, Longleaf, Lowlands, Marsh View Pitch & Putt, Red Fox

Championship Courses

Evans Prairie Country Club

In addition to the 42 Executive Courses there are 13 Championship courses in The Villages, the newest being the 18-hole Southern Oaks Championship course. Southern Oaks is the first championship course in The Villages south of 44, and at the time of this writing, 54 more holes of championship golf are on the drawing board for this new/future area.

The Villages Championship courses are immaculately kept, and are both fun and in some cases very challenging to play. Some of them were designed by the games biggest names in golf like Arnold Palmer and Nancy Lopez.

Most of these courses have 27 holes, but as I mentioned, Southern Oaks and a couple others (Tierra Del Sol and Orange Blossom Hills) have 18 holes. Residents of The Villages are automatically "members" of these courses as well, but unfortunately they are not free to play.

Championship Course Locations

Spanish Springs Area (North of County Road 466)

Glenview Champions, Hacienda Hills, Nancy Lopez Legacy, Orange Blossom Hills, Tierra Del Sol

Lake Sumter Landing Area (Between County Road 466 and 466-A)

Cane Garden, Havana, Mallory Hill, Palmer Legends

Brownwood Area: (Between 466-A and State Road 44)

Belle Glade, Bonifay, Evans Prairie

New and Future Areas (South of State Road 44)

Southern Oaks

What does it cost to play?

To give you some idea of what the cost is to play these courses at the time of this writing, on the low end Resident Members could play Orange Blossom Hills from June through December after 3 pm for $12, or on the high end play Belle Glade in January through May for $64.

If you plan on playing a lot of golf, it might make sense to look into upgrading your Resident Membership to a Priority

Membership. Priority golf memberships are available at 2...3...4...or all Championship courses. Priority membership gives you access to priority tee times and reduced greens fees.

Plus you are allowed to use all the country club pools and spas, and get a few other benefits. Choosing all of the courses will cost you $925/year for a couple.

For more details on the membership options available to you in The Villages visit:

golfthevillages.com

Requesting Tee Times

Residents are able to *request* a tee time up to 7 days in advance of when they want to play, however tee times are only actually *assigned* three days in advance of the day of play via the Automated Tee Time System.

Your tee time request can be made by using the automated tee time system, (available by phone or online through TheVillages.net) 4-7 days in advance of when you wish to play. If it is between 1-3 days in advance of when you want to play, you can use the automated tee time system to make an actual reservation. There's also the option to call the course you wish to play on the day of to see if they have any open tee times.

It's important to note that it's not a "first-come, first-served" kind of reservation system. Instead it is based on Placement Points (assigned to each golfer in your party based on yours/their membership level, eg: priority member, resident member, etc.) and Reservation Points (based on the number of tee time reservations you've obtained in the last seven days.)

After you move here you'll want to attend what's called the "Good Golf School" which will familiarize you with the ins and outs of the tee time system and how to use it.

You can also check out the Golfing in The Villages brochure here:

golfthevillages.com/golf-in-the-villages/GolfingIntheVillages.pdf

Most people think that with all of the courses available here, getting a tee time should be easy, but that's not always the case, especially during the busy season. The Villages is doing what they can by continuing to increase the number of courses available, but despite their efforts there are still times when you won't be able to play the exact course you want, exactly when you want to.

Practice Facilities

Sarasota Aqua Range

Practice makes perfect right? If you're serious about improving your golf game, you're going to want to put in some time on the range and the practice green.

The Villages currently has four practice facilities. These are located at Palmer Legends, Glenview Champions, Nancy Lopez Legacy, and the Sarasota Golf Practice Center. Both Nancy Lopez and the Sarasota Practice Center have aqua ranges.

In addition, practice greens are available at all championship courses, and most executive courses.

Specialty Golf

In addition to the Marsh View Pitch & Putt which falls under the Executive golf umbrella, The Villages has introduced a few other specialty courses to the mix. So far, these courses include the Fenney Putt & Play (at Fenney Recreation Center), and Clifton Cove Putting Course (at Ezell Recreation Center).

In 2022 the Jubilee Putting Course, Mickylee Pitch & Putt, Richmond Pitch & Putt, and First Responders Putt & Play are expected to open, and other specialty courses are planned for the new/future areas being developed.

The Villages Golf Academy

The Villages Golf Academy has a knowledgeable staff of PGA and LPGA instructors standing by to assist you in improving your game. They can work with anyone from pure beginners to the most advanced players and everyone in between.

The Villages Golf Academy offers group lessons, private lessons, club fittings, and more.

Tennis in The Villages

With golf taking most of the spotlight, tennis is kind of like the red-headed stepchild of The Villages. I say that because when compared to golf, pickleball, softball, and a few other more popular activities, there's really not much focus put on it. Even when you look at The Villages' website it's hard to find information about tennis.

While many of the recreation centers have tennis courts and you can find a number of tennis events listed in the weekly Recreation News publication, there are really only two country clubs with tennis in The Villages: Glenview Champions Tennis Club and Nancy Lopez Legacy Champions Tennis Courts.

Glenview Champions Tennis Club is considered the true home of tennis in The Villages, and is home to The Villages only tennis pro shop. It has won awards in the past from various tennis publications such as "Tennis Facility of the Year". Glenview Champions has 6 hydro-grid clay courts, lockers and showers, swimming pool and spa (shaped like a tennis racket), and again, a full pro shop. The number there is 352-753-1317 if you want to reserve a court or just get more information.

Nancy Lopez Legacy Champions has four similar hydro-grid soft courts and they sit next to Oasis Grill and Lopez Legacy Country Club pool. Court requests are made through the ACR system by calling 352-753-4653, or if you need a court reservation on the day of play, you can call the Glenview Tennis Shop at 352-753-1317.

Check out golfthevillages.com/tennis/index.asp for more information.

12

RECREATION

Nationally accredited by the Commission for Accreditation of Park and Recreation Agencies (CAPRA), The Villages Recreation Department services 100+ Regional, Village, and Neighborhood recreation centers, 100+ swimming pools, 3,000+ resident lifestyle programs and clubs with a full and part-time staff of over 600 employees and more than 3,000 volunteers.

Most of the activity takes place at the more than 100 recreation centers spread throughout the community. There are three main types of recreation centers:

Regional Recreation Complexes (RRC) are the biggest class of recreation centers, and typically consist of meeting rooms, arts & crafts rooms, a theater, pool and other outdoor facilities.

Village Recreation Centers (VRC) are a little bit smaller and consist of meeting rooms, a card room, billiards hall, kitchen, pool and outdoor facilities.

Neighborhood Recreation Areas (NRA) are even smaller still and usually contain a pool, bocce court, shuffleboard court and a horseshoe pit. Neighborhood Recreation Centers are also where you will find the postal stations for each neighborhood.

Laurel Manor Recreation Center

For information on the individual recreation centers throughout the community and everything the Recreation Department puts together visit:

districtgov.org/departments/Recreation/recevents.aspx

Fitness Centers

If you are going around the state looking at other retirement communities, most of the community clubhouses (akin to the recreation centers in The Villages) will have some type of fitness center.

But that's not really the case here in The Villages, with a limited number of exceptions. The following recreation complexes do have fitness centers, called "Fit Clubs":

Mulberry Grove, Laurel Manor, Colony Cottage, SeaBreeze, Rohan, Fenney, and Ezell.

There is an additional fee to use these "Fit Clubs", and memberships are available in 1, 3, 6, 9, and 12 month intervals. At the time of this writing, a one year membership for one person is $363.49.

The other option, which some regular gym-goers choose is to join MVP Athletic Club, which has locations in Spanish Springs and Brownwood. At the time of this writing the membership fee starts at $65/month.

mvpsportsclubs.com/mvp-athletic-club-brownwood/

Clubs and Organizations

As I mentioned, there are now more than 3,000 recreation department sanctioned clubs and organizations in The Villages.

Whether you are looking for ways to express a personal passion like painting or dancing, searching for a social circle that loves the same card games you do, or just want a reason to stay active during your retirement, there is something for everybody here.

In fact, most residents find more interesting clubs than they could possibly keep up with, so you might actually want to be careful that you don't overcommit yourself.

You can probably imagine some of the predictable clubs and activities that are available. But what are some of the more interesting clubs and activities that you can find in The Villages? Here are some examples:

Art & Writing Clubs

- Anybody Can with Watercolors
- The Village Clayers
- Grown-Up Coloring
- Glass Fusion
- Sketching Made Easy
- Rock Painting
- Wannabee Writers
- Writers 4 Kids
- Writers of the Villages
- Zentangle Mindful Drawing

Craft Clubs

- Basket Weaving (Seriously!)
- Crochet Addicts
- Eye of the Needle Stitchers
- Fabric Fun Arts
- Happy Hour Quilters
- Hooks & Needles
- Paper Crafting in 3D

- Scrapbooking Nite Owl
- Stampin Fools
- Vintage Sewing

Book Clubs

- Christian Women's Book Club
- Comic Book Collectors
- Jane Austen Plus Book Club
- Mystery Lovers 2
- Poetry Discussion Workshop
- Science Fiction Fantasy
- True Crime Book Club
- World War II Book Club

Dancing

- Ballroom Basics
- Belly Dancers / Gypsies
- Carolina Shag Dance
- Country Partner
- Hula Hands in Aloha
- Line Dance for Exercise
- Night Fever Dance
- Polish Folk Dancers
- Village Squares

Games

- Bunco Fanatics

- Chess Mates Tournament
- Darts for Couples
- Dirty Uno
- Friendly Friday Cribbage
- Fun Social Bridge
- J's Jokers Social Cards
- Mah-Jongg Maniacs
- Mexican Train Dominoes
- Pinochle Cards – Double Deck
- Pub Trivia Game
- Scrabblers

Hobbies & Interests

- .45 Sidekicks
- Beatlemaniacs
- Bonsai Workshop
- Dynamic Dogs
- Geocaching Club
- Home Brewers Club
- Karate 4 Life
- Master Gardener Speaker
- Model Railroad Club
- Photography Workshop
- Sailing Club
- Scuba Diving Club
- The Village Bicycle Club
- The Villages Classic Automobile Club
- The Villages Republican Club
- The Villages Griller & Smoker Club

- Wine Talk
- Woodworkers' Club

Music & Theatre Clubs

- Acting Out
- Bagpipe & Drum
- Barbershop Chorus
- Country Music Lovers
- Harmonica Band
- Jazz Improv
- Karaoke Fun Timers
- Native American Flute
- Not So Famous Players
- Peace, Love & Ukulele
- Songwriters' Showcase
- Villages Musical Theatre
- Windsong Ensemble

Sports & Exercise Clubs

- Archery Club
- Badminton Club
- Bocce Buddies Breakfast
- Hot & Spicy Pickleball
- Masters Tennis Club
- Mindbody Vinyasa Yoga
- Stickball Club
- Table Tennis Club
- Villages Fencing Club

- Walk Away the Pounds
- Women's Softball Club
- Zumba for All

Joining a club can be as easy as contacting the club and finding out what steps you need to take to become a member. Be aware though that some clubs are full and/or have waiting lists to get in.

For a great list as well as information on contacting these clubs and groups visit:

districtgov.org/images/ClubsListing.pdf

Other Sports and Activities

If I went over every sport offered or activity put on by the Recreation Department, this book would be hundreds of pages longer. You can learn about all of the great things they offer online at:

districtgov.org/departments/Recreation/recreation.aspx

Here are just a few sports and activities you'll learn about there:

Pickleball

Pickleball is one of the fastest growing sports in the country, and is especially popular in senior communities.

The Villages, boasting around 200 pickleball courts, has been called the Mecca of Pickleball and was named the #1 Place to Live for Pickleball by Masters Athlete Magazine. Leagues, tournament and recreational players of all skill levels occupy the community's courts year-round.

Pickleball is played on a badminton court with the net lowered to 34 inches. Players convey a perforated plastic baseball (similar to a whiffle ball) across the net with wood or composite paddles. Like tennis, singles or two-player teams can play the game.

Pickleball is wildly popular because it can be played by seniors (some of whom no longer play tennis due to injuries) while still offering a fast-paced physical and mental challenge. Growth of the sport, can in part, be attributed to Snowbirds who learn the sport in Florida during the winter and then introduce it in their hometown.

Pickleball clinics are held regularly in The Villages and the community has several pickleball clubs, and certified instructors.

You can learn more at: pickleballcommunity.com

Dragon Boat Racing

One of the fastest growing and exciting activities that you will find here is Dragon Boat Racing.

There are a number of club teams that emphasize different levels of competitiveness. Based on your fitness level and preferred training schedule, you can surely find a team that you will fit in with.

A Dragon Boat is a long, skinny canoe-shaped boat. The front of the boat is made to resemble a dragon's head, and the back of the boat looks like a dragon's tail. The crew of the boat each use individual paddles to propel it forward.

Traditional Dragon Boats are built for 22 people. This includes 20 paddlers, one drummer at the front of the boat, and one sweeper at the back of the boat. The drummer beats a drum in order to help the crew synchronize their paddling; he is tasked with speeding up and slowing down the paddling as needed. The sweeper is the person who is steering the ship. He uses a sweep oar as a small rudder to control the direction of the boat.

The rowers in Dragon Boats use a simple paddle, instead of the typical oar that you would find in most competitive racing boats. They paddle the same way any single person in a canoe would paddle. This makes Dragon Boat rowing very simple to learn, yet very difficult to master, which is exactly why it is so popular among villagers.

Softball

Buffalo Glen Softball Complex

Baseball might be America's Pastime, but Softball is The Villages' Pastime. There are hundreds of teams that compete across The Villages. With that amount of interest, there are leagues and teams open for any skill level. There are highly competitive traveling teams, as well as relaxed leagues that focus more on the social aspects of the game. If you have ever had the desire to play ball, there is a team for you located in The Villages.

The softball program at The Villages is organized and managed by the Recreation Department.

The Knudson Softball Field is located on the historic side north of HWY 441 next to Paradise Regional Recreation Center. The Saddlebrook Softball Complex has four fields and is located just off of Buena Vista Blvd near The Villages Polo Fields. The Buffalo Glen Softball Complex, also with four fields, is on HWY 446 near The Villages Charter High School. Opened in 2015, the Soaring Eagle Softball Complex on Morse Boulevard just north of State Road 44 has two softball fields. Last but not least, the Everglades Recreation Complex has four softball fields, bringing the total of softball fields in the community to 15.

You can learn more about the various softball leagues available at:

districtgov.org/departments/Recreation/softball.aspx

Fishing

Because of the year-round warm weather, there is almost never a bad time for fishing across all of Florida. Some might not know it, but there is also an abundance of great fishing located right here in The Villages.

When fishing at one of the many great locations around The Villages, it is important to make sure that you are following all of the guidelines set forth by the Villages Community Development District. These guidelines were put in place to ensure that fishing in The Villages will be a great experience for years to come.

The most important guideline to follow is that every fisherman over the age of 16 must have a valid license from the Florida Fish and Wildlife Conservation Commission. Children under 16 are not required to hold a license, and neither are residents over the age of 65 provided that they have proof of their age.

While there are many great fishing locations in The Villages, there are also some locations where fishing is prohibited.

It is important that you are aware of these locations and respectfully avoid fishing there. Fishing is not permitted in Lake Sumter, or anywhere that "No Fishing" signs are posted.

The Villages Community Development District specifies that fishermen are required to respect any private property rights around fishing areas. They also state that practicing catch and release is a requirement for fishing in The Villages.

Get more information, as well as maps of popular fishing spots at:

districtgov.org/departments/Recreation/fishing.aspx

Bicycling

In 2014 The League of American Bicyclists awarded The Villages the status of a Silver level Bicycle Friendly Community and in 2018 they upgraded The Villages to Gold level, meaning the community meets specific standards of engineering, education, encouragement, enforcement, evaluation and planning related to cycling. At the time of this writing, The Villages cycling community is making a push for Platinum level.

The Villages was the first Senior community to ever be awarded the Bicycle Friendly Community designation.

The Villages has over 100 miles of paved pathways that cyclists share with golf carts and pedestrians. The various bike clubs in The Villages have over 800 members, and there are thousands more riders who aren't members of clubs.

For more information check out:

thevillagebicycleclub.com

slbikeclub.org/

FloridaTandemClub.org

Swimming

The community is also a spectacular place for swimmers and anyone who enjoys spending their time by the pool.

With more than 100 pools to choose from, there is no shortage of options, and all of the facilities are kept in immaculate condition, just as residents have come to expect. All of the pools throughout the community are temperature controlled to make sure that the water is comfortable for everyone. There are also three different types of pools: sport pools, neighborhood pools, and family pools.

Sport Pools

The sport pools are incredibly popular among the more active residents. At the most basic level, these pools are sized and kept ready for those who enjoy swimming laps. Sport pools are also used for many popular water activities like water volleyball, water aerobics, and various other competitive events.

One of the groups that utilizes the sport pools is the Villages Aquatic Swim Team. This coed swim team is made up of residents from ages 50-99 that get together to practice several times a week. The team travels to meets across the state as well the country, and they're also known for having regular competitive showdowns with the Villages High School Swim Team.

Visit their website at: villagesaquaticswimteam.com

Neighborhood Pools

If you are more interested in relaxing by the pool than exercising in the pool, the neighborhood pools will provide exactly what you are looking for. These quiet and peaceful pools are for adults only. They provide a great place to get together and relax. Many residents can be found reading books, sunbathing, or even napping around their local neighborhood pools.

Family Pools

The family pools that are located throughout the community are the exact opposite of the neighborhood pools. These pools offer residents a great place to bring their visiting children and grandchildren. Swimmers of all ages are welcome to come and play in the family pools, which are filled with noise, splashing, and fun!

As with most everything here, the community provides its residents with nearly unlimited options when it comes to swimming pools. No matter what type of pool experience you are looking for, there are a handful of pools that will meet those requirements, and odds are pretty good that there is one nearby!

The Villages Senior Games

With a focus on fun and participation, The Villages Senior Games take place each year in the spring. Villagers compete in a number of events such as archery, 3-on-3 basketball, billiards, bowling, fencing, golf, pickleball, sand volleyball, swimming, table tennis, track and field, and more.

From there, the top competitors have opportunities to go on and compete at the state and national senior games, and every year Villagers bring home some impressive hardware from those events.

Camp Villages

Camp Villages is a year-round program that allows grandparents to spend quality time with their grandchildren. Camp Villages offers a wide variety of events for all ages and interests.

Monthly and special Spring Break and Winter holiday activities, as well as multiple summer sessions are offered.

You can learn more at:

districtgov.org/departments/Recreation/campvillages.aspx

Dog Parks

We are now up to 6 dog parks in The Villages:

- Paradise Park – Located on the east side of the original golf cart bridge
- Mulberry – Located adjacent to the fitness trail near the Village of Springdale
- Brinson/Perry – Located at 1231 Bonita Boulevard
- Atlas Canine Recreation Park - Located at 3513 Moyer Loop
- Dudley Canine Park – 2470 Fenney Way (South 44)
- Rupert Canine Park – 5743 Parkyn Path (South 44)

These are leash-free parks with fenced in areas for both small and large dogs. Amenities like water and waste stations are also available. The parks are open from 7 am to dusk.

More dog parks are on the way.

The Enrichment Academy

Years ago there was a program called The Villages Lifelong Learning College, created to provide residents a forum for intellectual stimulation and exchange and to enhance their awareness and involvement in life. Offering classes all year, with new courses beginning each month, the motto of the college was "No tests, grades, pressure. Just Fun."

Unfortunately in 2016, a lawsuit brought on behalf of hearing-impaired residents led to the demise of The Villages Lifelong Learning College.

But Villagers are not the type of people to let a beloved program just vanish without a fight. From the ashes of the Lifelong Learning College, a similar program, The Enrichment Academy was born in 2017. The Enrichment Academy is run by the Recreation Department.

From their website:

> "The Enrichment Academy, provides and operates a variety of fee based extra-curriculum courses that enhance and expand learning opportunities for residents and general public. Course curriculum complements the existing resident-led lifestyle and recreation services offered in the recreation facilities, providing even more choices to fulfill

our residents' passion for learning. The Enrichment Academy is committed to helping participants acquire knowledge for growth in mind, body or spirit."

The first Enrichment Academy classes began in the Fall of 2017 and included 125 classes on various topics in the areas of writing, language, history, art, dance, science, and technology. The current course catalog lists hundreds of available classes, seminars, talks, and other opportunities.

Learn more at: theenrichmentacademy.org

13
DINING, SHOPPING, AND ENTERTAINMENT

A large majority of dining, shopping and entertainment available to residents is concentrated in the existing three town squares, but there are also several other major shopping plazas that are important dining and shopping destinations as well. Let's take a closer look at each area.

Spanish Springs Area: Everything North of County Road 466

Spanish Springs Town Square

One of the (currently) three town squares in The Villages, Spanish Springs opened in 1994 and has a southwest flavor.

With adobe-colored shops surrounding a central meeting space, complete with viga-studded walls and a gazebo, Spanish Springs resembles a traditional plaza like one might find in Santa Fe – with the fountains and palm trees adding a Florida twist. Main Street winds around the integrated, mixed-use commercial area, providing access to a variety of shops, restaurants and offices.

Spanish Springs Fountains

Here are just a few of the restaurants, shops, and businesses in Spanish Springs:

- Banner Mercantile (The Villages Logo Store)
- Talbot's
- Patchington
- MVP Athletic Club
- The Villages Insurance
- Cal's Barber Shop
- The Corkscrew Winery
- Margarita Republic
- Augustine's 1812 House
- Panera Bread
- Dunkin Donuts

- World of Beer

While the offices, restaurants and shops draw residents to the square, classic car fans congregate in Spanish Springs each month during their "cruise-in" and Villagers turn out for live entertainment nightly. Spanish Springs has free entertainment every night, plus, parades and special celebrations throughout the year, from Cinco de Mayo to Halloween.

The Rialto Theater was the first of three movie theaters in The Villages. It closed for renovations in early 2020, then covid hit, bringing progress to a halt. As of this writing, it has not reopened and many residents are wondering if it ever will, considering the changes that the movie industry has been undergoing since the pandemic.

One other popular dining and entertainment venue located in Spanish Springs was Katie Belle's. Sadly it closed for good in 2020 shortly after the start of the pandemic.

Other places to dine and shop in the Spanish Springs Area:

- Buffalo Ridge Shopping Center (Walmart, Bealls, Dollar Tree, Petsmart, Marshalls/Homegoods, Red Lobster, Olive Garden, Bonefish Grill, and more)
- Mulberry Grove Plaza Shopping Center (Publix, Bealls Outlet, Beef O' Brady's, The Back Porch, and more)
- La Plaza Grande Shopping Center (Publix, Winn-Dixie, Belk, Ace Hardware, City Furniture, and more)
- Rolling Acres Plaza Shopping Center (Target,

Michaels, Petco, Carrabas, Outback, TJ Maxx, Ross, Fiesta Bowl, and more)
- Southern Trace Plaza Shopping Center (Publix, Havertys Furniture, Ace Hardware, IHOP, Culvers, and more)
- Spanish Plaines Shopping Center (Publix, Walgreens, First Watch, and more)

Sharon L. Morse Performing Arts Center

For years one of the biggest complaints people had about the entertainment venues in the community was that they were not big enough or new enough to draw some of the bigger acts and performers.

That changed when Church on the Square, a beloved Spanish Springs landmark that had about 770 seats, closed in late June 2013 to undergo a major renovation and was turned into what is now known as the Sharon L. Morse Performing Arts Center.

The new facility seats more than 1,000 people comfortably and is considered a state-of-the-art performing arts center by most who visit. Past performers and performances include Willie Nelson, Clint Black, Styx, Kenny Rogers, Kenny G, and the Broadway Hit Kinky Boots.

Check out the impressive schedule of performances coming soon to what is being affectionately called "The Sharon":

thesharon.com

Studio Theatre at Tierra Del Sol

Some smaller performances also take place at the Studio Theatre at Tierra del Sol. Considered an extension of the Sharon L. Morse Performing Arts Center, the Studio Theatre seats about 120 people, and its season runs from late September to April each year with four productions running approximately 130 total performances.

Savannah Center

The Savannah Center is a favorite among residents for its exciting entertainment lineup. World famous performers take to stage here, as well as national touring shows - with seating that can accommodate just over 850 guests.

You can see a full list of upcoming shows at Savannah Center as well as other venues throughout the community at:

thevillagesentertainment.com

The Villages Polo Field

Polo is a sport that you might not expect to find in a retirement community, but the Morse family has a love for the game, and so here it is. With a polo stadium in their "backyard," Villagers turn out en masse for the matches. They fill the stands, line the field with lawn chairs and tailgate (from their golf carts) before the action. It seems that once exposed to this fast-paced equestrian sport they become instant fans.

Polo has been a part of The Villages for the last decade. The Villages hosts Spring and Fall matches, and draws some of the largest crowds in the US, with more than 30,000 spectators a year.

The polo field also plays host to the The Villages Balloon Festival, Open Air Concert Series, and more.

thevillagespoloclub.com

Lake Sumter Landing Area: Everything Between County Road 466 and 466-A

Lake Sumter Landing Market Square

The second town square to be built in The Villages, Lake Sumter Landing Market Square, opened in 2004, and combines shops and services and provides an area for performances and community events, but this time with the look and feel of a small seaside village, complete with a waterfront and a lighthouse. There is live entertainment every night, and many special celebrations throughout the year.

Lakeshore Drive runs along Lake Sumter and connects with Old Camp Road to encircle the shopping and recreation area.

Lake Sumter Landing Lighthouse

Here are just a few of the restaurants, shops, and businesses currently in Lake Sumter Landing:

- Van Heusen
- Caribongo
- G.H. Bass & Co.
- City Furniture
- The Purple Pig
- Curve's
- The Villages Insurance
- Gar Vino's
- Bravo Pizza
- Chop House at Lake Sumter
- Sonny's BBQ
- Johnny Rockets
- Lighthouse Pointe Bar & Grille

Lake Sumter Landing is also home to the 120-room boutique hotel, The Waterfront Inn which combines old Florida charm with modern amenities and luxury.

waterfrontinnvillages.com

The next time a famous politician comes out with a book, catch up with them (or at least buy the book) at the Barnes and Noble in Lake Sumter Landing. Over the years the bookstore has had visits from Glenn Beck, Newt Gingrich, Mike Huckabee and Sarah Palin, and Donald Trump Jr.

The second of three movie theaters, Old Mill Playhouse, is located here and was the first theater to reopen after the pandemic. Old Mill Playhouse is also home to Lazy Mac's Taco Shack and Tequila Bar which offers a casual dining experience with comedy performances and live music.

Other places to dine and shop in the Lake Sumter Landing Area:

- Colony Plaza Shopping Center (Publix, Bealls Outlet, Cal's Barber, Walgreens, Sakura, PDQ, Fiesta Grande Mexican Grill, and more)

It may look like the Lake Sumter Landing Area is slim pickings as far as other shopping and dining options go, and while that may be technically true, Pinellas Plaza and Sarasota Plaza are just on the other side of 466-A to the south, and Southern Trace Plaza and Buffalo Ridge Plaza are just across 466 to the north, so it's not quite as bad as it may seem on paper.

Brownwood Area: Everything Between 466-A and State Road 44

Brownwood Paddock Square

Brownwood Paddock Square is the third town square to be built in The Villages. The theme of Brownwood is "Old World Florida" and takes residents back to a time in the 1800's when Florida's cattle hunters and cowboys roamed the state.

Brownwood, which opened in October 2012, is located in the Southwest corner of The Villages, west of Buena Vista Boulevard and north of County Road 44.

Sculptures at the entrance to Brownwood

Here are just a few of the restaurants, shops, and businesses currently in Brownwood Paddock Square:

- Tommy Bahama

- Raymond James
- Brownwood Jewelers
- The Villages Golf Cars
- Woof Gang Bakery & Grooming
- City Fire
- Five Guys
- Bluefin
- McAlister's Deli
- Scooples
- MVP Athletic Club
- Nail Saloon

Brownwood is also home to The Villages Grown Brownwood Market. The Villages Grown uses an innovative growing complex with controlled environment greenhouses and state of the art processing facilities to grow a wide range of produce like lettuce, microgreens, herbs, tomatoes, radishes, and cucumbers right in The Villages' own backyard. Just hours after harvest, the produce is available at The Villages Grown Brownwood Market, local Publix grocery stores, and even on the menus at some local restaurants.

thevillagesgrown.com

Just like the other two town squares, Brownwood is also home to nightly entertainment, and festivals such as the yearly Strawberry Festival, Blueberry Festival, and more.

One of the most popular weekly events in The Villages has to be the Farmer's Market hosted at Brownwood Paddock Square. At this market you can find dozens of local vendors selling everything from freshly baked breads, to locally grown organic produce, to hand-made goat's milk soap, and more.

The farmer's market at Brownwood runs year-round every Saturday from 9 am to 2 pm.

Next door to Brownwood you'll find The Brownwood Hotel and Spa, a AAA Four Diamond hotel and conference center that opened in 2020. The property also features a Wolfgang Puck restaurant.

brownwoodhotelandspa.com

Next to the hotel is the Advanced Center for Healthcare at Brownwood that I will talk about more coming up in the chapter on healthcare.

thevillageshealth.com/care-centers/center-for-advanced-healthcare-at-brownwood/

Other places to dine and shop in the Brownwood Area:

- Grand Traverse Plaza Shopping Center (Publix, Flipper's Pizza, Dickey's BBQ, and more)
- Lake Deaton Plaza Shopping Center (Publix, Piesano's Stone Fired Pizza, Walgreens, and more)
- Pinellas Plaza Shopping Center (Winn-Dixie, Walgreens, Square 1 Burgers, and more)
- Sarasota Shopping Center (Walmart Neighborhood Market, Quest Diagnostics, and more)

New and Future Areas: Everything South of State Road 44

Eastport

In the "planning and dreaming" stages at the time of this writing, Eastport will be located between the future Southern Oaks bridge and Central Parkway which was previously known as 470.

The developer is considering this area the "new center for the overall planned community", so I'm sure they will be putting a lot of focus and effort into making it great. Eastport will combine the town square concept with a regional recreation complex, golf, entertainment, shopping, and dining all into one location. It should be a very happening place!

The focal point will be Central Lake, a 1000 meter lake that will host dragon boat races and all kinds of other recreation. A waterside stage is also planned for concerts and entertainment. Current plans call for a recreation center with the a 20' high-ceiling gym, indoor and outdoor pickleball, a softball complex, a new hotel, a dog park, tennis and platform tennis courts, an executive golf course, a driving range and teaching academy, and more.

I don't know whether or not The Villages will ever build what will truly be considered The Villages' fourth "town square" even though that terminology has been used loosely in talking about Eastport.

As I mentioned, Eastport will...more than The Villages has ever attempted before...combine recreation, golf, retail, entertainment and dining into one location. I think it's a smart change that keeps pace with what new and future residents will be looking for. I'm not sure they've come out and said it yet, but I wouldn't be surprised if there were apartments available in or very close to Eastport as well.

When I think back to the completion of Brownwood and how long it took The Villages to fill all of the available commercial space, the high vacancy rate gave the impression that there wasn't a whole lot for residents to enjoy there, even though there really was quite a bit. Considering the "western" theme that Brownwood has, some compared it to a "Wild West Ghost Town" and it gave many newcomers pause when considering buying in surrounding neighborhoods. I can see why The Villages would want to take a different approach going forward.

Sawgrass Grove

While Eastport is a few years away, the first major dining, entertainment, and recreation spot to open in this area will be Sawgrass Grove. Nearing completion at the time of this writing, Sawgrass Grove is a multi-use area that combines recreation, golf, entertainment, a marketplace, and food in one location.

At the time of this writing, the Ezell Recreation Complex and Clifton Cove Putting Course are open at Sawgrass Grove. A box car stage has been put in place for the outdoor entertainment area, and things will get really exciting once McGrady's Restaurant & Pub, and the Sawgrass Grove Marketplace open.

The Marketplace will feature another location for The Villages Grown, Frenchy's Wood-Fired (pizza), Willy's Original (smash-burgers, sandwiches and salads), Little Fin (casual seafood), and a high-end aged beef and fine foods butcher.

Other places to dine and shop in the New/Future Area right now include:

- Magnolia Plaza Shopping Center (Publix, Villages Golf Cars, Willie Jewell's BBQ, Foxtail Coffee, and more)
- Edna's on the Green (a fun beer and wine bar nestled next to a golf green in the Village of Marsh Bend, with plenty of outdoor seating, a variety of food trucks and live entertainment)

And there's plenty more coming in the future, including Fenney Plaza, Warm Springs Plaza, and more.

The Villages Gourmet Club

One of the great things about The Villages is that there are now more than 100 restaurant options to choose from. The website of The Villages Gourmet Club features reviews of hundreds of restaurants not only in The Villages, but also in the surrounding areas. You might burn a lot of calories carting around in The Villages, but you won't go hungry (or thirsty).

thevillagesgourmetclub.com

14

HEALTHCARE

The Villages, recognizing the important role that healthcare would play in attracting those aged 55+ to their community, have tried their best to be on the leading edge as far as the types of care, types of facilities, and quality of service are concerned.

The stated goal of The Villages as far as healthcare goes is to be recognized as "America's Healthiest Hometown". Over the years they've tried really hard to be a leader when it comes to healthcare for seniors. Sometimes they've succeeded, and sometimes they've failed, but they keep moving forward.

The Villages Hospital

One of The Villages founder Harold Schwartz's last missions was to see a hospital built in the community before he died. In fact, he was so confident in the mission that he erected a billboard with a picture of himself pointing to a vacant lot with the words "I'll live to see The Villages Regional Hospital (TVRH) right here", and he did.

TVRH opened in July 2002, and Schwartz passed away at the age of 93 on December 22, 2003. Today, it is a 307-bed acute care hospital that has more than tripled in size since opening. Unfortunately it has not always enjoyed the best reputation among residents, patients, and healthcare rating agencies.

In 2019 it was one of 282 hospitals to receive a single star rating from the Centers for Medicare & Medicaid Services, which looks at more than 4,500 hospitals across the country and rates them based on a number of factors like safety of care, readmission rates, patient experience, and timeliness of care. This led to outrage among residents who packed meetings with hospital leaders demanding improvements.

In late 2019 a partnership with UF Health was announced, and in January of 2020, UF Health took over the hospital which is now named UF Health The Villages Hospital.

UF Health Shands Hospital in Gainesville is a five star rated facility, and is known as being one of the best hospitals in the state, so hopes were high when UF came in to take over The Villages Hospital.

UF Health The Villages Hospital is now rated two stars, which is a step in the right direction I guess. With Covid-19, most hospitals were just trying to keep their heads above water in 2020-2021, so to have made any improvement over that time counts for something.

As I think is the case with just about any hospital, you'll hear both good and bad things from people depending on the experiences they had. One of the complaints you'll hear most about this hospital is that ER wait times can be on the longer side, especially during the "season" (roughly November to April) which just so happens to coincide with cold and flu season. Go figure.

Another complaint I've heard recently is that if you have younger kids or grandkids visiting, UF Health The Villages Hospital might not be the best place to go, depending on what the issue is. The reason for this, some people say, is that the doctors and nurses there are used to treating older patients, and don't have as much experience with children. Again, this is something you'll have to figure out yourself.

If you do decide to go elsewhere for your hospital needs, other hospitals are available in Leesburg and Ocala.

UF Health Leesburg Hospital

leesburgregional.org

Ocala Regional Medical Center

ocalahealthsystem.com

Freestanding Emergency Rooms

UF Health The Villages Hospital is way up in the Spanish Springs Area of The Villages, residents in the newer areas have to travel quite a way for emergency care. But in 2020, two freestanding Emergency Rooms opened in locations that are more convenient to residents in other parts of The Villages.

One is run by Ocala Health and it is located in Wildwood on 466A just west of Buena Vista Blvd. This facility has 11,630-square foot facility with 11 ER beds staffed by 30 full-time health professionals.

ocalahealthsystem.com/locations/trailwinds-village-er/

The UF Health The Villages® Hospital Freestanding ER is directly across from Brownwood Paddock Square.

The 25,000-square-foot facility is open 24/7 and is staffed by physicians, nurses and patient care technicians, and has 16 beds, two of which are inside of state-of-the-art trauma bays.

thevillagesregionalhospital.org/services/emergency-services/uf-health-the-villages-hospital-freestanding-er/

New "Medical Village" and Hospital

Plans are currently in the works for a massive "medical village" and new UF hospital in the new/future areas being developed. It is not yet clear exactly what will go in there, but assuming these plans come to fruition, the hope is that the new hospital will alleviate some of the overcrowding that UF Health The Villages Hospital sometimes experiences.

The Villages Health

In 2011, an interesting partnership between the University of South Florida (USF) and The Villages Health System (TVHS) was announced. USF kicked-off the initiative with a resident survey and study on the health of residents of The Villages. Researchers examined a variety of indicators, such as the incidence of diabetes and how residents view their own health.

USF, which is located in Tampa, hoped to use the information collected to recommend improvements, like urging restaurants to serve healthier meals or sending in more specialists to care for residents with heart disease.

USF physicians engaged the community and residents through monthly educational seminars and by participating in medical rounds with local physicians at area hospitals.

Unfortunately, this ambitious partnership is no longer in place, but a few years into their partnership, USF Health and The Villages announced The Villages Health, a unique healthcare concept designed to redefine how Villagers interact with their doctors and treatment centers.

A slow start to the financial success of this venture led USF to pull out of the partnership in 2014, but The Villages Health continues on without them.

The main idea behind The Villages Health is that it is community-based and completely focused on the patients it serves in The Villages. There is a strong emphasis placed on preventative care, which should lead to reducing the overall cost of healthcare for residents of The Villages.

One of the best aspects about The Villages Health is that its care centers are conveniently located throughout The Villages. This makes it easy for Villagers to get to and from their appointments. Imagine the convenience of having your doctor, who you have a personal relationship with, only a 10-15 minute golf cart ride away.

These care centers are brand-new, state-of-the-art facilities that have been custom designed to provide exceptional care for aging adults. At the same time, they are designed to blend into The Villages landscape, so patients will feel completely comfortable visiting the centers.

There are currently seven primary care centers and two specialty care centers spread throughout the community.

For more information about The Villages Health:

https://www.thevillageshealth.com

Health Insurance

One early controversy surrounding The Villages Health had to do with their limits on what kinds of medicare plans they would accept. Those over 65 years of age were required to select a Medicare Advantage plan approved by The Villages Health in order to receive primary care. At the time, the only plan approved was UnitedHealthcare Medicare Advantage.

This led a lot of upset patients to choose to find new doctors outside of The Villages and outside of The Villages Health instead of switching from a plan they were happy with and could afford.

Today though The Villages Health accepts a wider range of insurance and Medicare options:

Medicare Plans:

- United Healthcare Medicare Advantage (Primary & Specialty Care)
- AARP Medicare Complete (Primary & Specialty Care)
- Humana Medicare Advantage (Primary Care)
- Florida Blue Medicare Advantage (Primary & Specialty Care)
- Medicare and Medicare Supplement (Specialty Care)

Commercial Health Insurance Plans (All Primary & Specialty):

- UnitedHealthcare
- Cigna
- Florida Blue
- Blue Cross Blue Shield
- Aetna
- AvMed
- Multiplan and Private Healthcare System

You can and should check The Villages Health website for any updates or changes that may have taken place since the time of this writing.

The Center for Advanced Healthcare at Brownwood

Opened in 2020, the Center for Advanced Healthcare at Brownwood is a four-story, 240,000-square-foot ambulatory/outpatient medical center near Brownwood Paddock Square.

It is home to one of The Villages Health's Specialty Care locations, as well as several other outpatient providers such as Aviv Clinics, Florida Cancer Specialists, LabCorp, Lake Medical Imaging, and even a Walgreen's Pharmacy.

Designed to look more like a welcoming hotel rather than a sterile medical center, the Center for Advanced Healthcare at Brownwood is connected to the Brownwood Hotel and Spa, a AAA Four Diamond property.

thevillageshealth.com/care-centers/center-for-advanced-healthcare-at-brownwood/

VA Outpatient Clinic

If you qualify for Veterans health care benefits, there is a VA Outpatient Clinic in The Villages. The 99,000 square foot facility opened in 2010 and serves thousands of veterans that call The Villages home. Major medical procedures and hospitalization are not provided here as it is an outpatient facility.

If you need a major procedure or more specialized care than this facility can provide, you will be referred (or even transferred, if necessary) to another local facility or the VA Medical Center in Gainesville, which is only about an hour away.

For more information visit:

northflorida.va.gov/locations/theVillages.asp

Healthcare Outside of The Villages

You should not feel like just because you live in The Villages, that you absolutely must utilize The Villages healthcare options.

One's healthcare is such a personal thing, and there are plenty of other primary care doctors and specialists in the areas surrounding the community. Everyone should do plenty of research on doctors both inside and outside the community before you make any decisions.

HealthGrades seems to be one of the more popular websites these days for finding doctors in a particular area, so give that a try:

https://www.healthgrades.com

Public Safety Department

Hospitals, specialists, and clinics are only part of The Villages healthcare equation though. In the next chapter I'll tell you more about The Villages Public Safety Department (VPSD), but in this chapter on healthcare I wanted to mention the vital role it plays in keeping residents healthy.

The VPSD has achieved accreditation from the Commission on Fire Accreditation International. This accreditation places the department in a rare class of only a couple of hundred fire departments world-wide that have earned this honor.

If you are going to have a heart attack someday, you should hope that it happens in The Villages. According to the results of a year-long study done by The Villages Daily Sun, residents of The Villages are four times more likely than other Americans to survive a cardiac event.

Fast response times play a role. Most homes in The Villages are within 2.5 miles of a fire station, and the VPSD says that their average response time is around 4 minutes.

But another key aspect to the higher cardiac arrest survival rate are the CPR and AED programs they've put in place throughout the community. AED's are available at most of the recreation centers.

Thousands of residents each year are trained in the proper use of the AEDs as well as CPR, and some neighborhoods have even created their own AED programs.

15

CRIME AND PUBLIC SAFETY

If you were to ask any resident the top few things they love about the community, the words "low crime" are often included in their answers. And while the community does have a pretty low crime rate, crime does exist.

Each year the FBI compiles data on crime rates in all 22 Metropolitan Statistical Areas (MSA's) in Florida, and The Villages MSA consistently has the lowest crime rate. The most recent year to be reported is 2020, and in that year The Villages MSA saw just 1,817 crimes per 100,000 inhabitants.

You can see data on all 22 MSA's at:

floridaforboomers.com/safest-places-florida/

Most of the crime in The Villages seems to be alcohol-related, including DUI's and sometimes domestic disputes and battery. But, the community has had its share of thefts and other crimes.

I don't make it a top priority to keep a running tab of the crimes that occur each year, but here are a few of the crimes that have occurred in the past:

- A group of Polish and Russian gypsies were arrested for stealing jewelry and silverware from homes in The Villages.
- A Villages man was arrested after he physically assaulted a woman who was sitting in a chair he had saved at Spanish Springs Town Square.
- An employee of McCall's Tavern confronted two teenagers who were driving recklessly around Spanish Springs Town Square. The teens attacked the employee, and he died a week later from his injuries.
- A married Villages man was arrested for firing 33 shots into his neighbor's home after she declined his repeated sexual advances. He later admitted to having a crush on the woman. (Luckily no one was injured
- An employee of an electrical contractor stole rings valued at $13,500 from a home he was working on in The Villages to feed a prescription pill addiction.
- A 60-year old Villages resident entered the VA Outpatient Clinic armed with an AM-15 rifle, at least two additional magazines containing 26 rounds of ammo each, and a 9-mm handgun. After confronting a Dr. in an exam room, a series of struggles ensued. The suspect's gun was discharged multiple times, but thankfully nobody was hit. The gunman was restrained by clinic staff and patients before being arrested by police.

I've told people all along, first impressions aside, The Villages is just like any other place with a population of 130,000+ people. There are always going to be criminals out to take advantage of such a high concentration of middle to upper class unsuspecting victims, and sometimes, even residents themselves fall off their rocker and do crazy things.

As one resident put it to me:

> "The Villages has over 130,000 residents. It's a cross section of America and much of the World. Are we really without any of the problems faced by other municipalities?"

Absolutely not, and the bigger it grows the more apparent that is to those who are paying attention.

In the past, much of what happens has gone unreported by the local media for various reasons which makes it really tough for residents, let alone prospective future residents, to get a handle on how much and what kind of crime problems The Villages really faces. This has changed recently with websites like Villages-News.com coming online and covering this stuff, but not everybody knows where to look.

Basically my goal is to let new and future residents know that just because you live in or plan to move to what some people describe as "Disney World for adults", you should not let your guard down. The same goes for wherever you decide to call home...not just The Villages!

Who Patrols The Villages?

As I've mentioned, The Villages spans three counties and dips into various cities like Wildwood and Lady Lake, so there are a mix of law enforcement agencies that patrol The Villages and that depends on where you are.

But the bulk of it is in Sumter county and served by the Sumter County Sheriff's Office.

Public Safety Department

The Villages has its own fire department, which is run through The Villages Public Safety Department. The department has nine stations, and more than 150 firefighters, paramedics, and other uniformed personnel.

Because their stations are strategically placed throughout the community, they've been known to have an average response time to fires, car crashes, and other emergencies of just over 4 minutes.

Ambulance services have always been contracted out to other public and private agencies, but a plan is being developed for The Villages Public Safety to take on this role starting in 2022.

Community Watch

Community Watch is a division of The Villages Public Safety Department. On-duty 24 hours per day, 365 days per year, their stated mission is "to provide a safe community for residents and visitors by being the watchful eyes of the community".

Although not a law enforcement agency, they work very closely with the local law enforcement agencies that service The Villages community. Paid community watch employees collectively drive more than 1.2 million miles per year, and are supposed to patrol each neighborhood Village twice a day. We'll talk more about the gate system in a moment, but Community Watch has cameras on all neighborhood gates and monitors them 24/7 from a dedicated dispatch/communications center. In addition, 20 or so of the gates in The Villages are staffed by gate attendants, and Community Watch is responsible for managing them.

Is The Villages *Really* a Gated Community?

Lots of people heading to Florida for retirement are interested in gated communities. But does The Villages qualify to be called a gated community?

The short answer is no. The longer answer is that although The Villages has over 100 gated entrances spread throughout the community, because the roadways are public roads, access to the individual neighborhoods cannot be restricted. Non-residents can just pull right up, press the red button on the call box to raise the gate arm and proceed on through.

Even though they are not really secure, the gates do serve the purpose of slowing vehicle traffic in and out of neighborhoods, and they likely keep some percentage of would be looky-loo's who don't realize how easy the gates are to bypass out of the neighborhoods, so that's something. The fact that video surveillance is in effect at all gates recording vehicles as they enter and exit and capturing license plates acts as a further deterrent.

As I mentioned, around 20 of the gates are staffed with gate attendants, about half of those are staffed 24 hours a day, and the other half are staffed from 6am to midnight. The job of the gate attendant is not to keep people from entering, but more so to serve in a customer service function, giving directions to those who need them, and in general smiling and waving cars through.

16

POLITICS

I'm a "vote for whoever I think is the best candidate" type of voter. I could care less about what party they're affiliated with. But some people moving to The Villages are political junkies, so this chapter is for them.

The Villages has become a popular campaign stop for aspiring candidates, especially Republicans. As you know by now, The Villages is located in Central Florida, but what you may not know is just how important the Central Florida area is to winning Florida.

The I-4 corridor (I-4 is the interstate that runs through the middle of the state from Tampa to Daytona Beach) divides the state into two fairly distinct sections. South of I-4 you have more densely populated areas, and to the north more rural areas. Approximately 40 percent of the state's voters straddle I-4.

According to a political science professor quoted in an article in The Washington Times:

> "We kind of laughingly call it the highway of heaven for the candidates, because if they win I-4, they win Florida."

So it's no wonder the politicians start visiting places like Orlando and The Villages early each election cycle in an effort to get the early momentum.

The demographic of people that make up The Villages is also a factor. It's no secret that a higher percentage of people age 55+ turn out to vote than some of the younger demographic groups. With The Villages you have a concentration of more than 130,000 people that are age 55 and over. If you're a politician going fishing for votes, you may as well put your boat in a stocked pond.

The Morse family (the developers) are big-time Republican party contributors. They've probably given more money to Republican party candidates than you and I will see in a lifetime, and before his passing, developer Gary Morse was co-chair of Mitt Romney's Florida finance committee in the run-up to the 2012 election.

Pro-Trump golf cart parades were common in the run-up to the 2016 and 2020 elections, and The Villages gave $250,000 to Donald Trump's inaugural committee after his win in 2016. While in office, President Trump visited The Villages in October 2019 to give a speech on Medicare, gave a shout out on Twitter in April 2020 to his "friends in The Villages" for how they dealt with the pandemic, and visited again in October 2020 for a campaign speech in the run-up to the 2020 election.

If you haven't figured it out yet, The Villages is considered a Republican strong-hold. That said, about 30% of voters in The Villages are registered Democrats.

Here are links to a few of the political websites in The Villages:

The Villages Republican Club of Sumter County

sumterrepublicans.com/the-villages-republican-club-2

The Villages Democrats

thevillagesdemocrats.com

Now that we've explored a few reasons why The Villages is a popular stop for candidates, let's take a look at some of the high-profile visits of recent years.

- George W. Bush made a campaign stop in 2004 then returned in 2010 to promote his book *Decision Points*. He is said to have been a close friend of developer Gary Morse and has reportedly visited The Villages several other times.
- VP candidate Sarah Palin made a campaign stop in the September run-up to the 2008 election and has since become a frequent visitor to The Villages whenever she has a new book to promote.. She has also graced the cover of The Villages Magazine.

- Caroline Kennedy, daughter of President John F. Kennedy, visited in October 2008 campaigning for Barack Obama.
- Rudy Giuliani visited while he was running for president back in 2007.
- Mitt Romney visited on multiple occasions while a presidential candidate, as well as to promote his book, and to campaign for Rick Scott when he was running for Florida governor. Lake Sumter Landing was the scene of Romney's infamous rendition of "America The Beautiful" which you can still find on YouTube.
- Paul Ryan visited in 2012 to campaign when he was on the ticket with Mitt Romney, and visited again in 2014 to promote his book *The Way Forward*.
- Vice President Mike Pence visited in the run-up to the 2016 election, and again in 2018 and 2020.
- And, as I already mentioned, President Trump visited twice while in office.

Politics certainly brought out the worst in people in the lead up to the 2020 election, and sadly, it was no different here in The Villages. Some confrontations between Trump and Biden supporters even made national news, and to an extent have continued well after the election.

17

COST OF LIVING

Far and away the most frequently asked question I get is some variation of:

"What does it cost to live in The Villages?"

The answer is not as straightforward as many would like, because everybody's situation is different, and figuring out one's cost of living is not at all like, say, inquiring about the price of a hotel room. But some folks seem to think it should be so easy and sometimes I wish it were.

In order to find out what YOUR cost of living in The Villages will be, it's going to take some serious effort and thinking on your part.

I know…the nerve of this guy, right? But I'm hoping that the information and resources in this chapter can at least help you arrive at a fairly accurate estimate of your potential cost of living.

A few disclaimers: prices are averages based on what I've heard, seen, experienced. Assume we're dealing with a $300,000 home when discussing housing related items. Prices change all the time.

I'd say well over half of the people posing this cost of living question have received an information package from The Villages and most of them question the accuracy of the monthly cost of living figures presented there.

If you've not received the package containing this sheet, it totals up the estimated cost of the amenities fee, sewer, water, power, trash, phone and cable, insurance, average taxes, and the CDD assessment and shows you a range of $783 to $1,261 per month to live in The Villages. (As of 2021)

While I do believe that most of their figures are accurate, they also leave out a lot of other expenses that make up ones cost to live in The Villages.

So let's take a closer look at figuring out your monthly cost of living and decide for ourselves whether or not living here is doable for you. What I'm going to do is present you with a list of costs that you might incur. Some of these might be ongoing monthly or yearly expenses (eg: lawn care) and others might be one time purchases (eg: buying a golf cart).

Again, it's important to keep in mind that many of these costs are not going to apply to everyone, I'm just trying to get it all down on paper and you can pick what's applicable and what's not. Also, assume the figures below are for a $300,000 home.

Buying a million dollar home in The Villages? Your costs will undoubtedly be higher.

Cost of Living Worksheet Download

I've also put together an Excel spreadsheet with a list of some of the expenses featured in this article. You'll want to plug in your own numbers but I at least wanted to get things started for you.

You can download the spreadsheet here:
insidethebubble.net/spreadsheet

*Important note: That is an automatic download link. Once you click it (if you're reading the ebook) or visit it after typing it into your internet browser the file will automatically download to your computer to wherever your downloads go. This will be different for everyone. Some people have a downloads folder. For others their downloads just go to their desktop. I often get emails saying "The link doesn't work." It works. You just need to find where the file was downloaded to on your computer or device.

Mortgage payment

I know many people pay cash for their homes, but many choose to carry a mortgage, even if it's just for tax deduction reasons. If you visit Bankrate.com you can calculate this one using your own figures but I used a $300,000 house, with 20% down, and a 30-year fixed rate mortgage at 3.1% and came up with $1,288 per month.

This cost alone doubles the seemingly attractive monthly cost of living estimate provided by The Villages, but again, a lot of people buying here do pay for their homes in cash and never get a mortgage, so a mortgage payment may or may not apply to you.

Homeowners Insurance

I think The Villages estimate of $70-$100/month here is pretty accurate. Of course you can adjust this up or down based on how much home you intend to buy accordingly. But, even though it likely won't be required that you carry it, I always tell people to get flood insurance too just in case. So let's call that an additional $400/year or about $33/month to be safe. You might also want to consider sinkhole insurance, but we'll explore that topic more in a later chapter.

Amenities Fee

This one is pretty straightforward. At $164 a month at the time of this writing this covers much of what makes The Villages such a draw. Things like golf on the executive courses, swimming, tennis, organized activities, 24 hour neighborhood watch and more. The amenities fee has been going up by a dollar or so the last few years, so depending on when you are reading this it might be a little bit higher. For historical reference, when I published the first version of this book back in 2008 they were $130 per month.

Property Taxes

The Villages estimates this at between $238 and $525 per month, depending on the price you pay for your home. In addition to the value of the home, the actual amount you pay in taxes will depend on whether you qualify for homestead exemption, and which county the home is located in. But for a $300,000 home count on paying between $3,000 and $4,000 per year, which works out to between $250 and $333 per month.

Sumter County, where most of the homes in The Villages are located, has a Property Tax Calculator on their website that you can use to estimate what your taxes might be:

sumterpa.com/tax-estimator/

Bond/CDD Assessments

An additional "non-ad valorem" tax you will likely see on your property tax bill, not included in the figure I just gave you, will be for the CDD bond and maintenance.

I'll explain more in the next chapter, but you'll likely have a CDD infrastructure assessment and a maintenance assessment. The infrastructure assessment can be paid off, and many homeowners choose to do that. You'll see some resales advertised with the statement "Bond paid". But regardless you'll always have the CDD maintenance assessment to contend with.

The Villages estimates this at between $129 and $220 per month, which is probably pretty accurate for a $300,000 home. But I've seen CDD assessments below $1,200 to more than $5,000 a year, so again, this is going to depend on what type of home you ultimately end up with, where it's located, if the bond is paid, and so on.

Utilities

In my opinion utilities are tough enough to estimate, let alone when you estimate them individually. You've got people that never set the thermostat below 80 thus they have a consistent power bill, but maybe they love their 30 minute showers leaving them with a higher water bill than others. So for simplicity's sake let's lump them into two groups: water/sewer/power/trash and cable/phone/internet.

For water, sewer, power, and trash collection The Villages estimates these costing between $182 and $262. I'd go a little more conservative here and estimate $300-$350 AND add another $100-$200 if you have a pool to cover the costs of running a pool pump. Add even more if you have an electric or gas pool heater.

The Villages cost of living estimates say nothing about cable, phone, or internet, other than that they are not included in their estimates. But I don't know too many people that get by without some combination of these services.

Of course some people may forgo a landline in lieu of using cell phones exclusively, and more and more are canceling cable and going strictly streaming. But no matter which combination of services you ultimately choose, I'd budget between $150 and $250 for cable, phone, and internet.

Landscaping

You might think cutting your own grass and trimming your trees and shrubs sounds like a good idea at first, but most people eventually agree it's either too dang hot or they are just too dang busy to keep up with it all. So most opt for a lawn service to come take care of this for them.

I'd estimate $50-$75/month for an average size house. Of course it's going to depend on the size of your lot and other factors, but we're shooting for averages here. Note that while you will get cut more in the summer and less during the winter, most services will charge you the same each month. It just helps them keep a steady cash flow and I think it helps the homeowner too so it's pretty easy to remember what to pay.

Trimming of trees/shrubs is usually additional. I think if you budget $40-$50/month here you'd be pretty safe.

Pest Control

Most people, especially those coming from up north, never think of this one. You're going to want to have your yard sprayed for pests, as well as the inside of your home too. Some companies recommend monthly service, others say you can get by with quarterly. In either case, expect this to set you back $80-100/month.

Termite Bond

No matter what type of home you buy, do not go without a termite bond. Count on paying at least $100-$200/yr. for this.

Exterior Maintenance

You might want to budget for having the outside of your home pressure washed once or twice a year, and painted every 5-7 years. Pressure washing will probably run $100-$200 per visit, and painting for a 1,800 sq. ft. home should be between $2,000 and $3,500.

Groceries

I'd say grocery prices in The Villages are pretty average for Florida. There's quite a bit of choice with Publix, Winn-Dixie, Walmart, etc., so the competition helps keep prices in check.

Drinks and Eating Out

Same for restaurant and drink prices. There are lots of choices, and the competition keeps the prices in line. You don't have to look too hard to find coupons and deals enticing enough for just about any budget.

But, because of the amount of choices, most of which are just a short golf cart ride away, residents find themselves eating out and/or socializing with new friends more than they ever have in the past.

So to be safe, add 20-30% on to whatever your budget is now for drinking and eating out, not because prices are higher, but because you will likely be doing it more often.

Golf

"Free golf for life" might just be the very thing that got your attention and attracted you to The Villages in the first place. But, it's not quite that simple.

There is a small fee for golf cart rental. You can also use your own cart and pay a trail fee either daily, semi-annually, or annually. You've got several options as it relates to Priority Championship Course Memberships, but on the high end they are currently $925 per couple (rates are less for singles) and this includes use of the Country Club pools and spas.

You also have to pay greens fees on top of this, though you do get a slight discount with this priority membership.

Golf Cart

This will likely be one of the first purchases you make after buying your home, and many even complete this purchase BEFORE buying their home! Prices, styles and options for golf carts are almost as varied as for homes. You can find used carts in the classifieds or in some stores for less than $2000 or you can spend more than $20,000 for a tricked-out custom cart. The choice is yours but don't forget to budget for this expense.

You'll also need golf cart insurance. Like anything else it's good to shop around. Ask your cart dealer or salesman for a recommendation. I've seen rates range between $60/year to more than $200/year.

Roadside Service

Like cars, golf carts get flat tires, dead batteries, etc. A couple companies offer roadside assistance for yearly fees ranging from about $35/yr. to $60/yr. depending on the level of service you'd like. Check out Kartaide and 24 Hour Cart Club for more details.

kartaide.com

24hrcartclub.com

Entertainment and Movies

You'll never be short on entertainment options in The Villages. You've got nightly entertainment in the town squares which is free. There are also ticketed shows, musical acts, Polo matches, etc. with ticket prices ranging from just a few bucks to more than $100+ depending on the act and the venue.

The Villages movie theater and ticket prices are currently $8.50 for residents showing a resident ID.

Newspapers

The Villages Daily Sun is currently $84/year. While you should probably subscribe just to keep up with daily events/happenings you're not going to see any hardcore news reporting. Because of this, many also get the Orlando Sentinel which is about $200/yr for a digital subscription or $360/yr for the print edition.

TheVillages.net

You can get golf tee times by phone, but most want the convenience of doing it online. If that's you, you'll pay $8/month for TheVillages.net. This also includes 2 @thevillages.net email addresses.

VHA/POA Memberships

I'm a strong proponent of joining these two organizations. After a while you'll notice they have different aims and viewpoints in many cases but both are worth being a member of. The Villages Homeowners Advocates (VHA) is just $25/household for 2 years, and the Property Owners Association is $10/household for 1 year.

Housewatch service

If you're going to be a seasonal resident you'll probably want to look into a housewatch service and these range from $35-$50/month depending on the level of service you want.

Various "One-Time" Costs

A lot of people fail to consider the many "one-time" costs they might incur when first moving to The Villages. Prices vary greatly for things like adding gutters, screening in your lanai, buying new patio furniture, adding decorative curbing, interior painting, and much much more.

Resident Parker Sykes, author of the epic post on my website "50 Things to Think About Before Buying a Home in The Villages" says that you can plan on at least $5,000 worth of this type stuff needing to be done at a minimum, and I'd agree. Just remember to take these into account when doing your budgeting/financial planning.

You can read that post here:

insidethebubble.net/50-things/

What did you come up with?

When I plug in some of the numbers above into a spreadsheet, I come up with a monthly cost of living (for me) of more than $4,000.

But don't let my number scare you. Maybe I factored in a little too much for golf, or maybe I plan to spend a little more on things like groceries and eating out than you. Adjust your figures accordingly!

18
COMMUNITY DEVELOPMENT DISTRICTS EXPLAINED

The Villages is made up of a number of Community Development Districts (CDD) responsible for a variety of functions that keep this place running smoothly.

Community Development Districts are special-purpose local governments. They are structured so developers can control the "district" and issue low-interests bonds. Funds from the bonds are then used to build infrastructure and amenities for the district residents.

The way CDDs work is that the CDD, run by a board that is chosen by the developer, issues bonds to pay for the infrastructure and other community improvements that new homeowners have to pay back over the course of a number of years, usually 20 to 30. The amount homeowners are assessed for this is typically added to their tax bill. This can be an unexpected extra expense if you are not familiar with the rules of the CDD.

CDDs are not necessarily a bad thing though, you just have to be careful and know what you are getting yourself into before buying in a CDD. The Villages would likely not have been able to grow like it has without the CDD framework.

The website for The Villages Community Development Districts provides a wealth of information on this topic, and has a lot of information you'll need after you become a resident.

districtgov.org

CDD Assessments

You will be required to pay both a CDD infrastructure assessment and a maintenance assessment. The infrastructure assessment can be paid off, and many homeowners choose to do that. You'll see some resales advertised with the statement "Bond paid". But regardless, you'll always have the CDD maintenance assessment to contend with.

The amount that you will have to pay in CDD assessments will vary based on which of The Villages CDD's your home is located in. These currently range from about $100 to over $500 per month. You can learn about all the different Villages districts at:

districtgov.org/yourdistrict/

Here's how the CDD infrastructure and maintenance assessments are calculated. For simplicity sake we'll use some nice big round numbers.

Let's say the infrastructure construction costs $10,000,000 and there are 1,000 acres within the District and the specific unit within the district your home is located in has 100 acres and there are 200 lots, the amount of the bond per home is $5,000.

The math would be $10,000,000 divided by 1000 acres = $10,000 per acre.

Your unit has 100 acres @ $10,000 per acre or $1,000,000 for your unit.

$1,000,000 divided by 200 lots = $5,000 bond per lot for your unit.

The annual CDD maintenance assessment is calculated in much the same way, except it is based on the annual budget established by the Board of Supervisors for each District, rather than the one-time fixed infrastructure cost.

Whether you are working with a new home sales agent from The Villages or an outside (MLS) agent, they should be able to tell you what the current CDD assessments are for each property you see.

As a prospective purchaser in The Villages, you are encouraged to review the budget. I also encourage you to attend a CDD Orientation which you can find out more about by visiting:

districtgov.org/school.aspx

IRS vs. The Villages

You may or may not have heard that years ago the IRS asked The Villages to pay back about $400 million in loans it received through the use of tax free bonds (a.k.a CDD's) to pay for the development and construction of just about everything in The Villages.

Golf courses, town centers, recreation facilities, and more were all built using this money. About the only thing the money wasn't used for was to build the homes that are in The Villages. In addition the IRS wanted nearly $3 million in back taxes.

While this type of arrangement is perfectly legal under Florida's Special Districts laws (there are more than 500 other special districts in Florida), the IRS challenged the legality of how closely the special districts are controlled.

In addition, the IRS also challenged the value of recreational assets sold to the community development districts. This issue had been going on for years and had been a concern for current and potential future residents, mainly wanting to know if it will be the residents themselves footing the IRS bill.

As of late 2015, positive progress had been made on this matter and the question as to the value of the recreational assets had been resolved, and there was an offer on the table from the IRS to settle the whole thing for $1.5 million. The District countered at $300,000. By the summer of 2016, after 8 long years, the IRS probe into the legality of The Villages CDDs was finally over.

In a letter to residents announcing the IRS decision, District Manager at the time, Janet Tutt, wrote:

"Although the IRS still believes the original bonds should have been taxable, and the Districts still believe the IRS analysis and position were incorrect, on July 14, 2016, the Districts received letters from the IRS that state: We have concluded that closing the examination without further IRS action supports sound tax administration."

Deed Restrictions

Another part of life within a CDD, and an important aspect of many communities like The Villages, is that living here involves following certain rules and regulations. In The Villages, these are most often referred to as "Deed Restrictions and Covenants".

Be sure to ask for a copy before you sign any purchase agreement, and make sure that the agreement is contingent on your understanding and approval of the Deed Restrictions and Covenants.

Restrictions do vary slightly from district to district in The Villages, but some of the common rules and regulations cover things like what kinds of changes you can make to the outside of your home (Important: you must usually get Architectural Review Committee or ARC approval to do this!), how many pets you can have, if you can have a fence and if so what kind, parking restrictions (eg: no Boats/RVs/Trailers can be parked at your home for more than 72 hours), and more. They also go into what the penalties are for breaking the rules.

You can easily see the restrictions for each individual district and unit in The Villages at:

districtgov.org/departments/community-standards/download.aspx

It may sound like a pain to have to follow these restrictions especially if you are coming from a community that doesn't have any rules like these. But as inconvenient as they may sometimes seem, these rules and restrictions do serve the important purpose of protecting your home values.

If you are going to pay a quarter of a million dollars or more for your new home here in The Villages, you want to know that someone is looking out for you and your investment.

19

FINDING YOUR HOME

Heard enough and ready to buy a home? In this chapter I'm going to walk you through the types of homes available in The Villages, the pros and cons of buying new and resale, and more.

First, let's start with a brief look at the different types of homes you'll find for sale in The Villages.

Types of Homes in The Villages

Over the years, The Villages has built a variety of homes styles, or "series" as they typically refer to them, including Patio Villas, Courtyard Villas (*this series includes Bungalow Villas and Cabana Villas*), Cottage Homes, Verandas (*a blend between Courtyard Villas and Designer Homes*), Designer Homes, and Premier Homes.

You can see examples of each at TheVillages.com website.

Patio Villas are going to be your smaller, less expensive options and Premier Homes account for the biggest and most expensive. All the other home series fill in the gap.

Construction materials vary between (and sometimes within) each series, with some homes being constructed of frame and vinyl siding, while others are concrete block or pre-cast concrete construction.

Keep in mind that over the years home classes and styles have changed, so the home styles The Villages is selling today does not necessarily reflect the full range of homes you might see in The Villages if you were to also look at resales.

The Villages does not have a "model center" per se like a typical community. So what most people do is look online at The Villages website to see where the open houses are and use that as their opportunity to check out the different floorplans.

Choosing The Right Size Home

Reader Dan asks:

> "One thing that I have heard from a number of people is they have moved several times since coming to The Villages. Any idea as to why this is such a common occurrence? I would rather make a good decision at the onset and be comfortable in our location choice within The Villages than move frequently like nomads. As we gather more information and maybe learn from others, I believe we can make our move to The Villages with full confidence in our decision."

Moving 2-3 times is common. I think it's less about location and more about size of home. It's different for everyone of course, but usually people start off too small, then they go larger, then they go smaller again. They think that they can deal with a smaller place in retirement but really can't and have to go big again. Then they get older and eventually decide they have to once again go smaller.

Now, as The Villages has grown and prices have grown right along with it, it hasn't really hurt these "2-3 time movers" financially. In most cases they've always been able to sell for more than what they paid. But if there ever comes a time where prices level off and don't grow so much, it could become costly to keep jumping around.

You might buy a house and even after 5 years not be able to eke out a profit after paying real estate commissions, closing costs, moving costs, etc. Definitely food for thought!

Understanding Lot Premiums In The Villages

Lot premiums are an additional charge that the developer tacks on to the price of a new home depending on where in the community a lot is located. Basically the way most new homes are sold these days is a builder will advertise their homes based on standard features and a "standard" lot, and anything they can use to justify an increase in price is a premium.

As you can imagine, the definition of "standard" varies widely.

So, in general, what kinds of lots in The Villages demand a premium?

- Oversized lots
- Lots that back up to a preserve
- Lots that back up to private land
- Golf front lots
- Golf view lots
- Cul de sac lots
- Corner lots
- Waterfront lots
- Lakefront lots

I've seen lot premiums in The Villages range from a few thousand dollars to well over $200,000 if you can believe it!

Now that's a pretty broad range, right. Why? Well when you consider that there are a few different types of homes in The Villages and you combine that with the several different lot types available, things can get out of hand pretty quickly.

Are Lot Premiums Worth It?

That all depends on how badly you desire a particular lot and how much it is ultimately worth to YOU…not the builder or any potential future buyer.

One agent I spoke with offered this advice:

> *"Is it worth it to have a house on the golf course or on the Lake or Pond. Of course. Will it add value to your home? Of course. Is it wise to pay the ridiculous upcharges for the premium lots that The Villages charges? NO! Find a resale that gives you what you are looking for without the high new bond and ridiculous premium lot upcharges."*

That's great advice if you can find a resale that fits your needs, but if not, you're sort of stuck with paying whatever The Villages is asking. If you don't, somebody else will.

Can Sellers Recoup The Cost of a Lot Premium?

This boils down to how much of a premium you pay and what a future buyer is willing to pay. Again, this from an agent I spoke with:

> "Rather than try to get back the premium the original owners paid, let's get top dollar for the home as a complete package. I have seen Realtors go crazy trying to figure out what The Villages charges for premiums...ultimately, it doesn't matter. A house is worth today what a house is worth today irrelevant of what was paid for it."

New Homes vs. Resale

When considering a home purchase in The Villages one of the first decisions you'll face is whether to buy a brand new home, or buy a resale (previously occupied) home. Your decision will depend on several factors including how quickly you need a home, your personal taste, and other factors.

Here are some pros and cons of both.

Pros of Buying a Brand New Home

One of the best things about a brand new home is that it is under warranty from the builder. If (almost) anything goes wrong while the home is under warranty, you won't be charged to have it fixed.

Plus, some people just have a mental fixation with "newness". They won't buy anything that someone has owned or lived in before. And that's o.k. This is your retirement, you should be able to decide this and no one else!

Also, another advantage of buying a brand new is that you may qualify for slightly better insurance rates because the home will be built to current building codes.

Cons of Buying a New Home

One of the cons of buying a new home in The Villages is that you will have to wait for the home to be finished, unless they already have the style of home you want in their inventory (commonly referred to as "spec" homes or "quick move-in" homes).

If you are on a tight schedule, or you do not want to find a temporary place to live while your home is being finished, you might want to pass on buying a new home.

Another potential downside could be location. Currently, all new homes are being built in the southern parts of the community. If you do not particularly care for the services and amenities in that area, you're kind of out of luck as far as buying new is concerned.

Pros of Buying a Resale Home

One pro of buying a resale home is that unless you have plans to do some remodeling before you move in, the home is ready to be occupied, and you know exactly what you're getting.

Most private home sellers are open to negotiation on price, depending on the market of course. The market at the time of this writing in late 2021 is very hot, and inventory of attractive resales is short, which gives buyers very little room, if any, to negotiate.

Cons of Buying a Resale Home

With a resale home you are not able to choose your décor such as tile and carpet, cabinets and countertops, or make any customization or personalization until after the purchase and, even then, not without a remodeling budget. It is what it is. Someone else has chosen the colors and materials, and their tastes may differ from your own. Something else to consider is that, depending on the age and construction of the home, your insurance may cost more.

Additionally, if you want the protection of a home warranty, it must be purchased separately at your expense, unless the seller provides one. Also, don't forget you'll need a home inspection, which you can read more about later in the book.

The Truth About Buying a Home in The Villages

I'd like to clear up a popular misconception that a lot of people have when they're thinking about buying a home in The Villages.

When you're working with the developer you've got a couple options:

1. You can choose a lot, choose a floorplan, and have your dream home built.

2. You can buy a new home they have in inventory with everything already picked out. This is the fastest way to get into a new home in The Villages. You are not stuck waiting for the home to be built. The downside though is that all the options and features for the house have already been picked out.

3. The last option you have when working with the developer's sales staff is that you can look at resales being marketed through the developer. There's nothing wrong with this of course, but as you'll learn below, this alone will not give you the "full picture" of what's available as far as resales go.

You should also know that in all of these cases, you're kind of on your own as far as representation is concerned. And I don't mean that to sound like you need to be constantly looking over your shoulder like somebody's out to get you, but you just need to be aware of this.

But here's the problem. You're probably asking: *"Well can't I just hire a Realtor or Buyer's Agent to represent me?"*

… and the answer is, when you're dealing with the developer, No, you can't. The developer won't work with outside agents.

See back before 2004 The Villages had all of the resales being marketed through them listed in the local MLS (the multiple listing service that all Realtors use). So back then you could have hired an agent and they would've been able to show you around and help you buy pretty much any resale on the market.

But in 2004 something happened and there was a disagreement between the developer and the MLS, and so The Villages pulled out of the Multiple Listing Service. So now, when you're looking at resales through the developer, you're missing out on seeing as much as 50% of the homes available as resales.

The percentage will vary from time to time of course…could be higher, could be lower…depending on a number of factors.

This 50%…these are homes where the owner decided they did not want to be represented by the developer, and did not want to have their home compete with the developers own inventory, and so they decided to hire an outside Realtor to list it and try to sell it for them.

Undoubtedly some of you might have your hearts set on buying a brand new home, and that's fine. But, even if that's the case, it will serve you well to know that if you're buying a new home, it's going to be located wherever The Villages happens to be building, which is currently down in the southern part of The Villages.

But maybe after checking out The Villages you fall in love with Spanish Springs or some other place in the northern part of The Villages and suddenly you find yourself making a lot of long golf cart rides to get to where you're going, when you could've … and maybe should've … checked out some resales closer to that area.

Here's an email I got from one of my readers about this very issue:

> *"I need to spend more time there with location in mind. All of the new homes seem to be miles away from the center of town and the developers agent only showed us the new areas. We are looking at renting for a month and checking out all of The Villages on our own."*

What he's saying is very true, so definitely keep that in mind.

A lot of people will put some serious thought into the location issue and decide that they're o.k. with a home that's a few years older in exchange for being in a more central location.

I could go on here, but I think you get the point of what I'm trying to tell you, and that's don't shortchange yourself by neglecting resales altogether, and certainly don't just work with the developer and miss out on a large percentage of resales that may be available.

So just to recap a little here, if you want to see all resales available you'll need to:

- Work with the developers sales team
- You need to look in the paper and online for For Sale by Owners
- and you need to find a Realtor who can show you the remaining 50% of homes listed for sale

For years readers have asked me to recommend agents to them, and I've always been reluctant because I just didn't know enough of the good ones to be able to make a confident recommendation.

But over the last few years I've taken the time to get to know and sort of "hand-pick" and "vet" a few of the top agents working in the community today, and if you'd like, I can personally introduce you to one of my trusted contacts who can help show you that other 50% of resales you can't see through the developer and just let you decide if any of those homes might be a good fit for you.

Learn more about how that works here:

insidethebubble.net/platinum/

List of Villages Neighborhoods

This list might come in handy when you are looking for homes and trying to figure out where certain neighborhoods are located. The Villages is comprised of several smaller neighborhoods that collectively make up The Villages. You should also be aware though that many of these neighborhoods can also be broken down further into smaller units.

In **Lake County** you'll find the Village(s) of Country Club, Del Mar, El Cortez, Hacienda, La Reynalda, La Zamora, Mira Mesa, Orange Blossom, Pine Hills, Pine Ridge, Silver Lake, and Valle Verde.

In **Marion County** you'll find the Village(s) of Briar Meadow, Calumet Grove, Chatham, Piedmont, Springdale, and Woodbury.

In **Sumter County, North of Road 466**, you'll find the Village(s) of Alhambra, Belle Aire, De Allende, De La Vista, Glenbrook, Hacienda, Palo Alto, Polo Ridge, Rio Grande, Rio

Ponderosa, Rio Ranchero, Santiago, Santo Domingo, Summerhill, and Tierra Del Sol.

In **Sumter County, South of Road 466**, you'll find the Village(s) of Amelia, Ashland, Belvedere, Bonita, Bonnybrook, Bridgeport at Creekside Landing, Bridgeport at Lake Miona, Bridgeport at Lake Shore Cottages, Bridgeport at Lake Sumter, Bridgeport at Laurel Valley, Bridgeport at Miona Shores, Bridgeport at Mission Hills, Buttonwood, Caroline, Duval, Hadley, Hemingway, Largo, Liberty Park, Lynnhaven, Mallory Square, Pennecamp, Poinciana, Sabal Chase, St. Charles, St. James, Sunset Pointe, Tall Trees, Tamarind Grove, Virginia Trace, and Winifred.

In **Sumter County, South of Road 466A**, you'll find the Village(s) of Charlotte, Collier, Collier at Alden Bungalows, Collier at Antrim Dells, Dunedin, Fernandina, Gilchrist, Hillsborough, LaBelle, Lake Deaton, Osceola Hills, Osceola Hills at Soaring Eagle Preserve, Pinellas, and Sanibel.

In **Sumter County, South of State Road 44**, so far you'll find the Village(s) of Bradford, Cason Hammock, Citrus Grove, Chitty Chatty, Dabney, De Luna, Desoto, Fenney, Hammock at Fenney, Hawkins, Lake Denham, Linden, Marsh Bend, McClure, Monarch Grove, Newell, Richmond, St. Catherine, and St. Johns, with many more to come.

Middleton by The Villages

The Villages is even working on a neighborhood for families who work and serve residents of The Villages, called Middleton. Middleton will have a new K-8 charter school, a state-of-the-art charter high school, plenty of shops, dining, and entertainment, as well as a wide variety of housing options, including apartments, townhomes, and single-family homes.

20

PAYING FOR YOUR NEW HOME

Roughly half of the people buying in The Villages pay cash for their home. But if you are buying a new home, plan to get a mortgage, and want the fastest and easiest mortgage experience, you should likely go through Citizens First Bank.

Citizens First Bank was founded by The Villages founding father Harold Schwartz back in 1991 specifically to meet the banking needs of residents of The Villages, and his great-granddaughter Lindsey Blaise serves as CEO today.

I don't know of any other bank more closely aligned and on the same page as The Villages closing department, which results in as seamless of a closing experience as possible for the homebuyer. I've heard from some buyers that Citizens First mortgage rates tend to be slightly higher than other lenders, but the convenience makes up for the higher rate.

citizensfb.com/lending/mortgages

However, if the best rate possible is what you are after, feel free to contact other mortgage lenders. Just make sure that they've had some experience closing loans on homes in The Villages. If there is even the slightest delay caused by your mortgage lender, The Villages will hit you with a hefty per day fee to delay your closing.

One outside lender that I've had real estate agents recommend to me is Justin Holloway of BB&T. His number is 352-314-3306.

VA Loans

The Villages attracts a lot of veterans, and some want information about VA loans. Unfortunately, as of this writing, The Villages will not allow a veteran to use their VA benefits to buy a new home, regardless of whether it is a pre-construction home or an already completed home.

The reason is that the VA inspection and appraisal process would slow down the production of new homes. This is not just a "Villages" thing, a lot of developers do not allow VA loans for the very same reason. So, if you plan on using your VA loan benefit to buy in The Villages, you *can* do that, but you will have to buy a resale.

Veterans of the United States Armed Services with more than 180 days active duty during peacetime, or 90 days during times of war may be eligible for a VA loan through Uncle Sam. In order to obtain a VA loan, the law requires that:

- the applicant be an eligible veteran who has available entitlement
- the veteran must occupy or intend to occupy the property as a home within a reasonable period of time after closing
- the veteran must have satisfactory credit
- and, the veteran and spouse must show stable income sufficient to meet the mortgage payments.

The advantages of VA loans are that they require no down payment, they are available from most lenders, and the VA prohibits lenders from requiring PMI, or Private Mortgage Insurance. The VA is guaranteeing the loan, so there is no need for a lender to require the veteran to pay for additional insurance against default.

On the downside, VA loans carry a one time funding fee ranging from one and a quarter percent to three percent, depending on the veteran's service, as well as other factors.

For more information on VA loans, visit:
va.gov/housing-assistance/home-loans/

Or, call the Florida VA Regional Loan Center at 1-888-611-5916.

21

PROPERTY, FLOOD, & SINKHOLE INSURANCE

In addition to the obvious need to protect your investment, the ability to get homeowner's insurance is of utmost importance when getting a mortgage on your property. No mortgage company will loan you money without you first having insurance on the property. In some instances your mortgage lender can even foreclose on the property if you fail to carry insurance. I have done my best to compile for you the facts and resources, as they now stand, to help you navigate the homeowner's insurance landscape in The Villages.

Current State of the Florida Property Insurance Market

Well before Covid-19 reached our shores, the Florida Property Insurance Market had been feeling ill. Some Florida homeowners are experiencing 20-40% property insurance rate increases, and some with older homes, particularly with roofs that are more than a decade old, have been dropped by their insurance carriers altogether.

I explain more in my other book, the Florida Retirement Handbook, but for our purposes here I'll just say that you can chalk most of the issues up to scams and unnecessary litigation. The good news is that these issues are on the radar of our state's elected leaders, and reforms put in place between 2019 and 2021 have eliminated some of the problems, but experts think it will take time to see if the recent legal changes will be enough to stabilize the Florida property insurance market.

Fortunately, I haven't heard of as many problems about insurance in The Villages as I have in other places. Let's hope it stays that way.

Getting Coverage

Presumably you now have homeowner's insurance on your current residence, wherever that might be. My first piece of advice is to ask your current insurance agent if their company writes homeowner's insurance policies in Florida.

If you are with a large national insurer with operations in Florida, the odds are good that they do write homeowner's policies in Florida. By doing this, you are taking the path of least resistance, and you will probably be able to get pretty decent rates through what are called "multi-line" discounts assuming you have other property such as cars, jewelry and the like already insured through them.

You are welcome to shop around and price out other insurers, but from what I've seen, if you are comfortable with the company you have now, switching carriers to save a few bucks usually isn't worth the hassle.

The Villages Insurance

If your current carrier does not write insurance here in Florida, or they do but you decide for whatever reason you want to shop around anyway, you might begin your search with The Villages Insurance, owned by the developer.

They offer homeowners, auto, life, and golf cart insurance and with several locations throughout The Villages, you would be hard-pressed to say there's a more convenient option available.

Visit their website at:

thevillagesinsurance.com or call 352-751-6622

Other Popular Carriers

While The Villages Insurance is probably the most convenient option, it can sometimes pay to shop around. Here are some other options that residents and real estate agents have recommended to me in recent years:

Thomas Insurance (352) 326-8021

HBS Insurance (Wendy Grabe) (352) 350-1422

All In One Insurance (Denise) (352) 314-3038

Blakely Insurance (352) 314-3700

Frank Slaughter Insurance Agency (352) 748-2221

Cash Value vs. Replacement Cost

When shopping for homeowner's insurance, there are various types of coverage available for you to choose from, including "actual cash value" and "replacement cost coverage". I've always been told, and I believe it to be true, that guaranteed replacement cost coverage is the type of coverage you should be after.

With an actual cash value policy, if you are insured for $200,000 and repairs to your damaged home cost $250,000 the insurance company will be covering $200,000. Guaranteed replacement cost coverage means that even if you are insured for $200,000, if your home is destroyed and it costs $250,000 to build at today's construction costs to be put back into use as it was before, then that's what the insurance company will pay.

This type of coverage will cost more, as you might imagine, but it provides the policyholder with much more protection. One way to mitigate the rise in your premium is to raise your deductible. When you raise your deductible, or the amount you pay out of pocket to file a claim, your yearly premiums will go down.

Windstorm and Hail Insurance

The insurance company that I've always used (State Farm) includes windstorm and hail insurance in their basic homeowners policy. I'm not sure if that's how every insurance company operates, but I know that most mortgage companies require this coverage. The rates vary based on where your property is located, what kind of roof you have, whether or not you have hurricane shutters or impact resistant windows, and so on.

But not all types of insurance you might want or need to consider here in Florida are automatically included, which brings us to flood and sinkhole insurance.

Flood Insurance

Sunken Ship at Lake Sumter Landing

There are two facts that most people do not know. First, flooding is the number one natural disaster in the United States; even properties not near water can be susceptible to flooding. Second, losses due to floods are not covered by your homeowner's insurance policy.

While flooding is not a major concern in The Villages, it has happened. The most recent example is the flooding that occurred when Hurricane Irma dumped more than a foot of rain on The Villages in less than 24 hours. Most incidents of water intrusion from that storm happened in the older parts of

The Villages, built in the 1970's and 1980's when standards for mitigating flooding were less stringent.

Arguments have been against golf courses for some negative effects they can have on the environment, but one thing that's neat about The Villages is that excess rainwater is actually channelled to the golf courses which are designed to flood if necessary in order to prevent homes from being flooded. After Irma, residents were actually without golf for about two weeks while all of the courses dried out.

The Federal Emergency Management Agency (FEMA) puts out "flood maps" that show which areas tend to be most prone to flooding. I often hear people ask, "is the property in a flood zone?" and usually people describing homes in low-risk areas will say "no, it's not in a flood zone." Well, the correct answer is that every property is in a flood zone. It's just a matter of whether it is in a low, moderate or high-risk flood zone.

Your real estate agent might be able to tell you which flood zone the property you are looking at is in, and there are a few online resources available to help you determine this (links at the end of this chapter). But it is your insurance agent who will use a Flood Insurance Rate Map or FIRM, to ultimately determine your flood risk. Be aware that federal law requires you to purchase flood insurance if you have a federally backed mortgage and reside in a high-risk area.

In my opinion, everyone, no matter where in Florida they live, should carry flood insurance which is available through the National Flood Insurance Program (NFIP). In most cases the insurance company that handles your regular homeowners insurance coverage will be able to help you secure this.

In an effort to keep the NFIP solvent, FEMA is rolling out changes that are supposed to go into effect right as this book goes to print in October 2021 that, in their words, "will fundamentally change the way FEMA prices insurance and determines an individual property's flood risk" and "delivers rates that more accurately reflect flood risk and ensure the National Flood Insurance Program will be here for this generation and generations to come".

The new changes go beyond considering simply whether a property is in a low, moderate, or high risk flood zone, and takes into account other variables like potential flood frequency, flood type, a property's distance to a water source, elevation, cost to rebuild, and more.

Before these changes, you could get $250,000 of building and $100,000 of contents coverage for about $420/year. According to FEMA, with these new 2021 changes about 20% of covered Floridians will see a rate decrease (though they don't specify how much of a decrease), 68% will see a $0-$120/year increase, 8% will see a $120-$240/year increase, and 4% will see a greater than $240/year increase.

For more information on flood zones, flood maps, and flood insurance contact your insurance agent or visit these websites:

floodsmart.gov

floodfactor.com

Sinkholes - What You Need to Know

Sinkholes are a fact of life in many parts of the country, not just Florida. Unfortunately, The Villages is not immune to them either. There have been several confirmed sinkholes in The Villages over the years, some just as recent as this year at Moyer Recreation Center.

Florida has more sinkholes than any other state. This is because in many parts of Florida, the ground near the surface is sitting on top of limestone. When underground water levels rise and fall, this limestone can dissolve and form holes. When the ground below is no longer strong enough to support the weight of what is on top, there may be a sinkhole. Sinkholes can happen anywhere, but if you research this topic on your own, most websites will tell you that North Central and West Central Florida are where they seem to occur most often.

For insurance purposes, it's important to distinguish between what's known as Catastrophic Ground Cover Collapse coverage, and sinkhole coverage. They are two different things.

Florida law requires all homeowners insurance policies to include Catastrophic Ground Cover Collapse (CGCC) coverage, but there is strict criteria that must be met for an incident to be covered:

1. The abrupt collapse of the ground cover;
2. depression in the ground cover clearly visible to the naked eye;
3. Structural damage to the building including the foundation; and

4. The insured structure being condemned and ordered to be vacated by the government agency authorized by law to issue such an order for that structure."

If a sinkhole occurs and any one of those four criteria is not met, the incident will likely not be covered by your insurance company. If you read those criteria again, you'll note that your home must literally be condemned and vacated for CGCC coverage to kick in. There have been efforts in the state legislature to change this but as of this writing nothing has made it out of the proposal stage.

Fortunately (in the case of safety) or unfortunately (in the case of your ability to collect insurance money to fix your home), most sinkholes do not cause enough damage to meet this criteria.

That's where optional sinkhole coverage comes in. Florida law requires all insurance companies writing policies in Florida to offer sinkhole coverage, typically as a separate policy or in a rider, and of course this will be at an additional charge above and beyond what your regular insurance costs. It's also important to note that if geological testing or an inspection reveals that sinkhole activity is present on your property or within a certain distance of it, the insurance company can decline to provide sinkhole coverage to you.

While actual geological testing can cost thousands of dollars, most insurance companies will simply send a representative out to do a walk around of the property and sometimes they'll come inside and inspect around windows and doors for signs of excessive settling before approving you for coverage.

To learn more about sinkholes, contact an insurance agent or visit:

floridadep.gov/FGS/Sinkholes

22
HOME INSPECTIONS AND WARRANTIES FOR RESALES

Home inspections and home warranties are two tools available to you that will help to ensure that the present and future condition of your new or resale home in The Villages is satisfactory.

Home Inspections

Before finalizing the purchase of a resale home, you should always have a home inspection done by a licensed professional. This point cannot be stressed enough. A home inspection could be the best money you ever spend. Home inspectors conduct a thorough evaluation of the home that can help you understand the condition that the house is actually in before you take ownership. Remember, that sometimes looks can be deceiving, and nobody likes unexpected surprises or costly repairs once they move in. Even if the house is fairly new and appears to be in good condition, you never know what could be hiding out of plain sight.

Most home inspections don't reveal much of anything, maybe faucets that need tightening, or caulking that needs to be done. The point of an inspection is not to convince you that so much is wrong with the house that you are discouraged to buy it. It is rather to give you an accurate depiction of the current condition of the house, as well as an idea of how certain things will hold up in the future.

When major items are found, such as a failing air conditioning unit, or bad wiring, the parties must look to the real estate contract to see who will be required to make the repairs. Home inspections typically cost anywhere from $200 and up, depending on the size of the home. After the inspection is complete you will be given a detailed report of all the inspector's findings, whether good or bad, usually accompanied by digital photos.

A typical home inspector will inspect the structural elements of the home consisting of the roof, outside and inside walls of the home, patios and driveways, as well as parts of the foundation if visible. They will go into the attic to inspect the trusses, the underside of the roof decking for water intrusion, and insulation. The systems of the home will be inspected including the electrical, HVAC, and plumbing systems. All appliances that are staying with the home are inspected and tested for proper operation, and usually a random spot check of electrical outlets, windows, and doors will be done.

Other items that a home inspection company might perform for additional fees include radon gas and mold testing, water analysis, and pool and spa inspections. Most home inspectors subcontract for a termite inspection that may be at an additional cost to you, but it is a very important part of any home inspection here in Florida.

Some home inspection companies in The Villages for you to look into are:

LabPro Home Inspections

Lon Barnaby

Cell: 352-552-0610

www.labproinspections.com

Comer Home Inspections

Tom Comer

Office: 352-323-9715

www.comerinspections.com

USA Home Inspections

Chris Ulrich, owner

Office: 352-450-3020

https://www.usahomeinspections.com

Southern States Inspection Services

352-622-0066 or 877-668-2411

AmeriSpec

352-867-7625

Hometeam Inspection Services

352-694-8201 or 800-459-8326

Also, ask your real estate agent or friends and family for referrals.

Home Warranties

If you are buying a new home from the builder, one of the advantages you have is that your home will come with a warranty provided and paid for by the builder.

But this doesn't mean that you're out of luck if you decide to buy a resale home. There are several home warranty options available to you, no matter the age or condition of the home you are buying.

Home warranties for average homes under approximately 5000 square feet will cost you between $300 and $400 dollars per year. You can renew these on a yearly basis. Most plans do not require an inspection of the property before they take effect. Depending on the company you choose and the specific plan you go with, an additional amount may be needed to warrant some items like the A/C, refrigerator, washer/dryer, and a pool or spa.

Typically covered items include the plumbing, electrical, and heating systems, water heater, most appliances, disposal, smoke detectors, and exhaust fans. You need to read the warranty contracts carefully to see exactly what is and what is not covered. For example, a warranty might cover your refrigerator motor, but not the shelving inside the refrigerator.

Should something that is covered by the warranty break down, there is usually a service call fee, anywhere between $40 and $80. Other than paying that, you will not be required to pay out any money for the repair or replacement of a covered item. Most home warranties are pretty simple to acquire, fairly inexpensive, and are usually worthwhile.

Some national home warranty companies to consider are:

American Home Shield

ahswarranty.com

Old Republic Home Protection

orhp.com

23

WALKTHROUGH AND WARRANTY FOR NEW HOMES

Since we just talked about inspections, should you get an inspection for a brand new home?

Some people do, but because the responsiveness and support you'll get from The Villages Home Warranty Department is typically pretty good, you can probably put off hiring an inspector for a newly built home, at least temporarily.

But what a lot of people will do is after 8-10 months of being in the home, and with a few months months left on their first year warranty, they'll have a home inspection done just to see if there's anything else that a set of trained eyes can catch wrong with the home that might need to be reported to home warranty before the first year is up. You'll see some companies even mention this in their marketing pitching "11th Month Inspections".

Contact any of the inspectors I mentioned in the last chapter or ask your friends and neighbors for recommendations.

New Home Orientation

The walkthrough, or new home orientation as it is sometimes called, is one of the most important phases in the purchase of your new home in The Villages. The walkthrough is a time for you to meet with your builder and let them acquaint you with your new home and all of its components.

Most builders have their own preferred order for how they want to take you through the house. If that's the case, let them take the lead. They've likely done this hundreds of times.

There's a great video on The Villages Home Warranty website that goes over some of the basics your builder will likely cover:

thevillageshomewarranty.com

If your builder doesn't have a preferred order, you might want to follow the order I've laid out in the following pages. The walkthrough is a time for you to give your new home the once over, looking for any issues not up to quality standards.

Allow Enough Time

Allow ample time to go through your new home. In my experience an hour or so is sufficient for average sized new homes. Also, leave any pets, kids, or curious friends and relatives at home. There will be plenty of time for them to experience and enjoy your new home in due time. The walkthrough is serious business and should be treated as such.

Here in The Villages, the walkthrough will usually occur a few hours before your closing, so there's no time to waste. Minimizing distractions is critical!

What to Bring

To ensure a successful walkthrough bring along a pen or pencil, a black permanent marker, a packet of neon green dots available at office supply stores, and a pad of legal paper. Understand that everything might not be perfect once you start the walkthrough. It's just the nature of home building that no matter how careful, the builder can't catch everything. But, if you follow my advice, the builder and his team will be in the position to get things corrected for you in a timely fashion.

As you find items not up to standards, place one of the neon green stickers I suggested you bring on the item and write it down on your legal pad or a punchlist provided by the builder, or both if you feel it necessary. Green dots can mysteriously disappear but if you write it down it can't be forgotten for long.

Breaker Box and Electrical System

You will of course be tempted to head for the front door and bask in the glow of your fresh new home. But not so fast. Let's cover some things in the garage first. The garage houses several important components of your new home and you should become familiar with them. The first item on the list is the breaker box. This is where the electricity that comes into your home is regulated. Your builder should show you where it is and how to operate it.

Make sure that each breaker has been clearly labeled for you. This will eliminate headaches down the road. Also, there should be some GFI outlets in the garage. Now is a great time for your builder to test those in front of you, and to show you how they work. Also, make sure they test the GFI outlets inside the home when you get in there.

Water Heater

Be sure to check the water heater. Most of the new homes in The Villages now come with tankless water heaters, and your builder should show you how to adjust the temperature controls.

Water Shutoff

The main water shutoff valve to the home will usually be located inside the garage or sometimes on the outside. Your builder may advise you to turn the water off if you will be leaving the home for days at a time. This is probably good advice, at least initially until you've lived in the home a while and made certain there are no leaky toilets or pipes.

Air Handler and Air Filter

The air handler, which distributes the heated or cooled air throughout your home, will usually be in the garage as well. Make sure your builder opens the filter door to show you how to change the air filter. Using the black permanent marker, make note of the filter size in a conspicuous place on the front of the air handler. You should change the air filter about every month for best performance.

Garage Door

While you're still in the garage, open and close the garage door to check for proper operation and make sure the remote controls work. If your garage door opener came with an outside keypad, ensure that it too works. In the event of a power outage you may need to open the garage door manually. Have your builder show you how to do that.

Kitchen

Once inside the home, the best place to usually start is the kitchen because there is so much to cover there. Make sure that there are no scratches on the kitchen countertops or cabinets. Open and close a random selection of cabinet doors to make sure they are working properly. Make sure the hinges are tight, and the cabinets aren't sticking or rubbing against anything as you are opening and closing them. Your builder should give you care and cleaning instructions for both your counters and your cabinets.

Turn on the kitchen faucet and set it to the hottest setting. Here we are checking to make sure that the hot water heater is working properly. As long as you've got hot water after what you feel is a reasonable length of time, you're doing just fine. Have your builder show you how the sink disposal works, and how to clear it if it gets clogged. Also have them show you where the individual shutoff valve is for the water in the kitchen as well as the locations of the GFI outlets.

Appliances

Examine the appliances that came with your home. First, examine the outside of them to make sure there are no scratches or dents. Accidents do happen during construction, but assuming you bought new appliances, and not scratch-and-dent specials, they should be in brand new condition. Turn the stovetop on, check that the burners are working, and then try heating the oven. Assuming everything is working thus far, start the dishwasher to run through a cycle. This is to mainly make sure that there are no leaks in the dishwasher, either when it fills or when it drains.

While the dishwasher is running do a quick check of the refrigerator. If there are integrated ice and or water controls in your refrigerator make sure they work. Don't use the first batch or two of ice; just discard it in the sink. Also, most manufacturers suggest running through and pouring out the first couple of gallons of water from the refrigerator. This is to make sure that the water line becomes clear of any debris that may have gotten inside during construction and installation.

If your home came with a microwave, also check to make sure it works. In the laundry room, start both the washer and the dryer if provided and make sure they are working correctly. Make sure the dryer vent hose is connected.

All of the appliance instructions and warranty information should be kept in one easy-to-access location. Some of them may have cards for you to fill out and mail in to the manufacturer to record your warranty.

Drywall and Flooring

Before leaving the kitchen, examine the flooring for quality. Also check the walls for any drywall imperfections and check the paint for any spots the painter may have missed. As you see things that don't meet your standards, write them down on the list and place a green dot on or near the problem area. This is so that the drywallers or painters know exactly where to look to correct the problem areas.

Continue your flooring and wall inspection throughout the remainder of the home. Don't forget to look up every now and then and inspect the ceilings.

Systems and Components

As you are going through the home, have your builder show you how various things work, such as how to set and control the thermostat, how to use the security system and intercom if there is one, and how to operate the central vacuum if you bought one. If your home has a fireplace, whether it is wood burning, gas, or electric, have the walkthrough representative show you how it works. Make sure you are given instruction booklets on each of these items and that you place them with your appliance booklets.

Bathrooms

Visit the bathrooms and check that the plumbing works. Again turn on the hot water, then the cold water to check the functioning of each. Be sure to check the showers and baths, as well as the sink. Water lines sometimes get reversed. Hot will be cold, and cold will be hot, but this can be easily corrected.

Flush the toilets and make sure they have adequate water flow and don't remain running long after you flush. Check the tile work inside the showers to make sure that there are no holes or gaps in the grout or caulking. You don't want water getting behind your tile in there. Examine the vanity tops for scratches and cabinets for loose hinges.

Exterior

Be sure to inspect the outside of your home as well. Your builder should familiarize you with where the hose bibs are located, the sewer cleanout, and anything else that is important. Make sure all of the exterior walls of the home are evenly painted, and do an inspection from ground level of the roof to make sure there are no shingles that look loose or out of place. If your home comes with a sprinkler system, you should be shown how to operate that.

Warranty

After you feel you've examined the home top to bottom and have made note of anything that is not satisfactory, you should have your builder go over any warranty paperwork that is given to you, so you have an understanding of what items in the home are covered and for how long.

When things settle down a little bit and you have some time, it can never hurt to read over all of the warranty information. This will help you feel more comfortable with the warranty claim and repair process should you ever need to go through it in the future.

The website again for Home Warranty is:

thevillageshomewarranty.com

There you can download helpful forms, care and use guides, and of course contact them for any warranty related needs or requests.

NEW HOME AND RESALE CLOSING PROCESS

The closing process for new homes in The Villages is pretty cut and dry. You'll typically do your walkthrough with your builder and then head to the closing. Most closings take just 20-30 minutes. Because they perform so many home closings each day, it's important that you show up to your appointment on time. I've read reports of fees being charged to people who had to delay and/or reschedule their closings.

Some people close by mail rather than having to arrange flights and timing it just right to be there in person. If you go this route, once you get to town you'll still meet with your builder and if there's anything amiss with the home you can report it to home warranty and get it taken care of.

Resale Closings

Closings on resales *could* take place at an attorney's office, but here in Florida they don't *have* to. It's usually up to whomever is paying for the title insurance, which is typically (but doesn't always have to be) the seller. Oftentimes the closing on a resale will take place at the office of a title insurance company.

Title Insurance Companies

Because of their importance in your real estate transaction, most title insurance companies provide closing services. It is very common for closings on property in Florida to take place at a title insurance company office. The title insurance company will act as a neutral third party to ensure that all terms of the contract have been met, and they will collect and disburse funds according to the terms of the contract.

What is Title Insurance?

Before the closing on your home, a title insurance company will conduct extensive research into public records, surveys, and other recorded documents to ensure that no party (other than the seller) holds an interest in or has a lien upon the property you are trying to purchase. According to the American Land Title Association, nearly one-third of all title searches reveal a problem with the title. Unknown heirs, divorces, tax liens, and fraud or forgery can cause title problems. Thankfully most can be resolved before your closing.

Upon completion of their research, the title insurance company issues an owner's policy to the buyer, and a lender's policy to the lender. Like I said, in most cases the seller will customarily pay for an owner's policy but, as with most other costs, this is negotiable. If you do end up having to pay for it, the cost will be $5.75 per $1,000 up to $100,000, and $5.00 per $1,000 thereafter. If you are financing, your lender will require you to pay for the lender's policy, but this does not cost very much. It will be usually be only a couple hundred dollars or less because you are getting what's called a simultaneous reissue credit with the owner's policy.

Typical Closing Costs

There are costs other than the sales price that are incurred in every real estate transaction. As the buyer, your share of these costs will typically range from 1% to 2% of the sales price. The closing costs that you pay will be a function of a couple factors including what you have negotiated in the real estate contract and whether or not you are getting a mortgage. Costs that are customarily paid for by the buyer include:

- Recording of the deed
- Documentary stamps on the deed* ($.70 for every $100 of the sales price).

*This is typically paid by the seller in a resale transaction, but I included it here because the builder often requires the buyer to pay this

- Documentary stamps on the mortgage ($.35 for every $100 financed)
- Intangible tax on the mortgage ($.002 times the mortgage amount)
- Lender's title insurance policy
- Taxes

- Prepaid interest
- Prepaid fees or dues, capital contributions, or transfer fees
- One year of insurance in full
- Appraisal Fee
- Underwriting Fee
- Flood certification fee
- And potentially more, depending on your unique situation

25

THINGS TO DO RIGHT AFTER MOVING HERE

Moving to The Villages, or anywhere for that matter, can be both a very exciting and very stressful time.

You put in a lot of work choosing the right place to retire, finding the perfect home for you, packing, unpacking, and more. By the time you're through your brain is probably fried and all you want to do is relax.

But once you've made it here, there are still a few things you should take care of as soon as possible to make sure you get the full amount of enjoyment out of The Villages and take full advantage of all the fine benefits you are entitled to.

File for Homestead Exemptions

Do you like saving money? I know I do. Luckily, Florida gives us a couple ways to save on our property taxes in the form of homestead exemptions, provided you meet certain residency requirements. But believe it or not, people forget to apply for these exemptions and end up paying more. You will not be one of these people right?

Every person who has "legal or equitable title (you own it) to real property (your home) in the State of Florida and who resides on the property on January 1, and in good faith makes it his or her permanent home is eligible for a homestead exemption."

Remember, you have to make application for the exemption between January 1 of the previous year and March 1 of the year you want the exemption. For example, for the 2022 tax year, you would have been able to apply for homestead exemption from January 1, 2021 to March 1, 2022.

When filing your homestead exemption for the first time, you will be asked to provide evidence that you are a legal resident, such as a voter registration card or a Florida driver's license. There is no need to reapply each year as long as you are in the same home. If you move, however, you will need to reapply.

If you are a part-time resident using your home in The Villages as a vacation home or second home, you will not be eligible for this exemption.

You can read more about whether you may qualify at the Lake, Sumter, and Marion County Property Appraiser's Office websites.

Join BOTH the POA and VHA

The Villages Property Owners Association (POA) and The Villages Homeowners Advocates (VHA) are two organizations that will help you get the most out of life in The Villages.

While many people choose to affiliate with one over the other, I always tell people to join both. Why?

To begin with, both organizations are good advocates for residents. Though they focus on different issues (the VHA is closely aligned with the developer, while the POA is more independent), it doesn't hurt to support both organizations. If nothing else than to stay in the loop and keep your finger on the pulse of your new hometown.

The VHA tends to play up "what's right" with The Villages, and the POA focuses on "what's wrong" or "what could be improved".

Another benefit besides staying informed, is that both the POA and VHA have partner programs which offer residents some good discounts from many of the local restaurants and businesses serving The Villages. Use just one or two of these discounts per month and you're easily paying for the cost of your membership.

poa4us.org

thevha.net

Attend a Golf Cart Safety Clinic - These are currently held at the Colony Cottage Recreation Center at 9:00 AM on the third (3rd) Wednesday Morning of each month. Learn safety tips, cart maintenance tips, and get insurance information.

Attend a New Resident Night

The Villages Homeowners Advocates mentioned above offers a newcomer orientation called "New Resident Night" on the 2nd Tuesday of each month (outside of holidays that happen to fall on this day) at 7 pm at Colony Cottage Recreation Center.

The VHA's New Resident Night is a great intro to The Villages and covers a lot of information about The Villages itself, as well as the VHA.

Attend "Good Golf School"

For a place well known for its abundance of golf courses, it's interesting to note that not everyone who moves to The Villages plays golf. For some, their move to The Villages will mark the beginning of a long obsession with the game.

The Good Golf School is not where you go to learn how to grip and swing a club though. It's where you go to learn the ins and outs of The Villages tee time system, with some basic golf course etiquette thrown in for good measure.

Whether you've been playing golf your whole life or if this is your first time, Good Golf School should be on your list of things to take in right after moving to The Villages.

To find out more and register, call the Tee Times Office at 352-750-4558

Good Golf School classes are held once or twice a month on Thursday mornings from 9am to Noon at Colony Cottage Regional Recreation Center.

CDD Orientation

Each week The District hosts an information session titled "Introduction to your Special Purpose Local Government". Here you will learn how the various services that support The Villages are run and learn what you need to know about each of them.

No need to sign up, just show up to one of the sessions which take place on the second and fourth Thursday of each month at 10 A.M at the District Office (984 Old Mill Run).

If you are still craving even more information after that, you could take the next step and attend the Resident Academy.

From the District website:

"The Resident Academy is an interactive program for residents who are interested in learning about their local government. Our ultimate goal for the Resident Academy is to alleviate the confusion, questions, or mis-information that exists throughout the community regarding the responsibilities and functions of the Community Development Districts.

During this program, participants will receive an in-depth look at the various District Departments and how they work together to make this the best community to live, work and play. Department Directors will also be available to answer questions or make appointments for those seeking additional information."

If you are interested in becoming a part of the Resident Academy, call the Customer Service Center at 352-753-4508 or stop by the office at 984 Old Mill Run. Due to the popularity of the Resident Academy, there is sometimes a waiting list to attend.

Meet the Neighbors

Last but certainly not least, don't be shy!

If you attend some of the events I talk about above, you're bound to meet some other people who, just like you, are new to The Villages and are looking to meet other newcomers.

But some of the first people you're going to want to meet after you move to The Villages are your immediate neighbors. Everyone is friendly in The Villages, so just walk up to the door of the neighbors on either side and across from you, extend your hand and introduce yourself. Who knows, you may have just met your next set of great friends.

ADDITIONAL RESOURCES

Older editions of this book included a list of phone numbers that residents might need from time to time, but The Villages Phone Book is now available online, so I'm going to save a few trees here and give you the link to that:

thevillagesphonebook.com

Frequently Used Numbers (All are area code "352")

The Villages Sales and Information: 753-6655

The Villages Home Warranty: 753-6222

District Customer Service: 753-4508

Public Safety: 205-8280

Automated Tee Time System: 753-4653

Entertainment Ticket Box Office: 753-3229

Frequently Used Acronyms

AAC - Amenity Authority Committee

ARC - Architectural Review Committee

BCDD - Brownwood Community Development District

CDD - Community Development District

CIC - Community Improvement Council

LSL - Lake Sumter Landing

POA - Property Owners Association

PWAC - Project Wide Advisory Committee

RLVG - Resident Lifestyle Volunteer Group

SJRWMD - St. Johns River Water Management District

SLCDD - Sumter Landing Community Development District

TEA - The Enrichment Academy

VCDD - Village Community Development Districts

VCCDD - Village Center Community Development District

VCSA - Village Center Service Area

VHA - Villages Homeowners Advocates

VPSD - Villages Public Safety Department

Made in the USA
Las Vegas, NV
11 May 2022